LAS MADRINAS

LIFE AMONG MY MOTHERS

Consuelo Matiella Viuda de Martínez
"Mamachelo"

LAS MADRINAS

Life Among My Mothers

Ana Consuelo Matiella

TRES CHICAS BOOKS

ACKNOWLEDGMENTS

The following chapters were previously published in the following journals:

"La Madrina" in *Connotation Press*
"La *Puta*" in *The Santa Fe Literary Review*
"La Malinche" in *Gravel: A Literary Journal*
"La Viuda" in *Compose, A Journal*
"La Novia" in *Clover, A Literary Rag*
"La Hija –(Milagro #1)" in *Adroit Journal*

Photographs courtesy of the author.

Cover photograph: Tessar

Banner illustration: Lance Sprague

Design: JB Bryan / La Alameda Press

Set in Janson with Posada titling.

ISBN: 978-1-893003-19-4

Tres Chicas Books
P.O. Box 417
El Rito, New Mexico 87530

CONTENTS

PROLOGUE

· · · · · · · · · ·

LIFE AMONG MY MOTHERS

As LUCK WOULD HAVE IT, I HAD MORE THAN ONE MOTHER. It took a lifetime for me to realize this. I took them for granted for so long, but looking back, there they all are. My world has been duly populated by women who loved, supported, mentored, guided and blessed me. It started with my mother, Emma Moreno de Matiella. She was a *cuentera*, a storyteller, or more accurately in the lexicon of the place where I grew up, one who makes things up.

She told me once, "I don't know how it works but sometimes when I don't know something, I just make it up and it comes true."

"The Gringos call it affirmations," I said.

She laughed. "Lies that come true."

I have often thought of my writing as telling lies about the truth and telling the truth about lies. I attribute this philosophy to my mother and her capacity to spin a tale.

Although she was uneducated by today's standards, she was brilliant in my eyes. She was witty and astute, observant and brave. She had something to say about everything. She never said, "I don't know." In today's jargon you would say she had personal power and that would be a good thing for a woman to have. But as her child I felt her power like a giant thumb and for a long time, perhaps until the day she died, I never felt successful in standing up to her.

For a long time, I felt like she simply had too much on me, making me feel small with her judgment, her certitude, her beauty, and her wit. She was a good mother sometimes, and sometimes she was a bad one, but lucky for me, she was not my only mother. I had other-mothers, *mis madrinas*. I needed them and they showed up.

This landscape that you are about to enter — mythical, insane and ovarian in nature — is the world according to my mothers.

I was born in Nogales, Sonora, Mexico and spent most of my time at my maternal grandmother's house on Calle Rosario. When I was six years old, my father moved us to the American side of Nogales so that we could be educated in the American school system, which he deemed to be better than the Mexican school system. I don't know how much better it was, but he succeeded in providing us with an American education.

They called the place Ambos Nogales because it was one community with a fence that divided the Mexican side of Nogales from the American side of Nogales. There were some notable differences between the two sides, but I didn't really notice until I left and someone told me that I came from two places, not one.

On the Mexican side, we had no TV, no air conditioning, no car once our mother dropped us off at Nana's, and no hot water. On the American side we had no bread man coming to deliver bread from a table he carried on top of his head, no washer woman to do the wash in the yard, no chickens, no pigeons, no goats to feed, and no man with a dancing monkey.

Several of these impressions of my life take place on Calle Rosario, in Nogales, Sonora, Mexico — a deeply rutted road that went up one side the sharp dry hill and down the other like the spiky back of a dragon. Several others take place *al otro lado*, on the other side — in Nogales, Arizona, on Perkins Avenue, a flat paved street that might have been in *Leave it to Beaver* and finally, in a haphazard chronology, there were a few impressions that led me from my native land in the Sonoran desert to my adopted home in Santa Fe, New Mexico.

As you read, you might feel a bit like Colette when she asked, "Where are the children?" Only you might ask, "Where are the men?" As a child, my world, whether on Calle Rosario or Perkins Avenue, was dominated by women from my mother to my *madrinas*, to Our Blessed Mother Guadalupe. It was a feminine world. The men, as my grown daughter used to say, were "MIA — Missing in Action." My father traveled for work and we only saw him on weekends and often drunk. My Tata, grandfather, the family mensch, died when he was 62 and I was three. (My Nana said it was because the good die young.) My twin uncles were in their teens when I was growing up on Rosario Street and not so dependable until they got older. And then there was Romeo, my eldest uncle who was a mensch like my Tata, but also on the road in my early years. He drove a bus for the Mexican bus company, Transportes Nortes de Sonora. So the men were out of town.

I have named these personal memories, "Life Among My Mothers," in honor and in gratitude for all my mothers, *las madrinas* who shaped me and showed me the different ways one can be a woman. Some of these memories are imprinted firmly and some of them elude me, but like my mother, I am a *cuentera* and whatever I didn't know, I made up.

I call these memories "impressions" because they are not unlike footprints left behind. These memories and impressions are about women and are based on a feminine lore. It is a lore from women and places that do not exist anymore. They only exist in the spirit and here, in my heart … *en mi corazón*.

Ana Consuelo Matiella

2015

Emma Moreno de Matiella

LA ROMANTICA

. . . .

THE ROMANTIC ONE

MY MOTHER TOLD US THAT WHEN SHE SAW MY FATHER for the first time, she fell madly in love. She described every detail. There was a dance at *La Cueva de los Leones* — the Lion's Club Cave, and she wore a yellow georgette dress that her mother had made; it was trimmed in brown velvet. Her brown suede high-heeled shoes matched her purse. The hem of the dress came right to the point that showed off the best angle of her shapely calf. He came sauntering across the dance floor. He was not tall, but he was so handsome it was shocking. He had blue eyes and beautiful white skin. His black wavy hair combed back made the blue of his eyes stand out and he picked her out from across the room. They danced a tango as everyone stopped and let them have the floor.

The Second World War had just ended and he was still in uniform; he was the son of Spanish immigrants; my grandfather had come with his young wife to Nogales in 1913 to build a cigar factory. A son of a prominent Spanish family was a good catch. My mother was of a more humble origin, the daughter of a working class family with no ancestral recollection of being anything other than Mexican.

My mother admitted to us many times that she was smitten by this handsome Spaniard in uniform, son of a cigar factory owner, who could dance like Fred Astaire. She told us over and over about that first dance, about how he promised to return in a month, to the day, and ask for her hand in marriage. That's the way we all got started.

In my most romantic moments, I keep this fairy tale encapsulated in an oval ornament that lingers gracefully in the hollow of my heart. When I am more pragmatic, I realize it could be something as rudimentary as a fabricated memory to sweeten the past. Nevertheless, it is a story of how my mother and father began our lives as something beautiful.

I remember how I loved to watch them dance. I wanted to go to the weddings and the lovely late afternoon *tardeadas* just to watch them glide across the floor. My father was a well-trained dancer, he reminded us with pride. During the war, while he was stationed in San Antonio, he completed a course in ballroom dancing at the Arthur Murray School of Dance. He found the perfect dance partner in my mother, who had beautiful light feet that could follow his every move. I remember fearing they would fall when their feet didn't touch the ground. They were airborne. They were so beautiful when they danced, they could fly.

I don't know when things went bad. I was a child and only kept track of their dancing and what my mother wore, but things did go bad. He was drinking too much and she begged him to stop. She tried everything, from withdrawing love to telling him what to do, back to telling him she didn't care. In my logic, if they could only go dancing, things would be okay, but I remember once watching my mother pulling my father out of the car in the dawny light of a New Year's Day, hanging him like a rag doll over our fence while she tried to open the garden gate. She was wearing the green goddess chiffon dress. (I had a name for each of my mother's "going out" dresses.) The green goddess had a flowing trail of chiffon over each shoulder, anchored by rhinestone clasps. Her shoes were dyed to match. She looked like a sad Barbie doll as I peeked out through the living room drape; I ran and got under the covers so she wouldn't notice that I was there.

There were many more rough spots and fewer and fewer dances and our family became a series of sad stories. It took years for my father to be consumed by alcohol and for my mother to develop a rare and terminal blood disease. She was 58 years old when she died. Before she died, she wanted to leave him, but I, using all the power of the eldest daughter, said no.

"Yes, it's true," I told her, "he is an alcoholic and yes, it's true that you have suffered, but if you leave him, he will die, and you said yourself he was an honest man, one of great intelligence and wit. A man of honor. You can't leave him when he's down, Mama. You just can't."

My mother didn't leave my father through the contentious and shameful road of divorce but through the tunnel of death that she illuminated with the strong conviction that there was such a force as the Holy Spirit. Right before she died, she was giving out photocopies of a prayer to the *Espíritu Santo* that she had clipped out of the *Nogales Herald*. She was not afraid of death, she said to me on various occasions; she was ready to go at the first call.

She spent a week in the hospital, going in and out of consciousness, and in one of her most lucid moments she touched her heart and said, "Me duele el corazón."

"Your heart hurts? Let me call the nurse," I said, getting up from the chair.

"No," she said, "not that heart, the other one. The heart of love. El corazón de amor."

I went to reach for her and she glazed over in that merciful coma. I rubbed her heart and said, "I'm sorry, Mama." It was not an apology. It was an acknowledgement of the pain she held in her heart.

Sensing that she was in the final stage of death, I called my sister in and we both said goodbye. "Bye, Mama, Mama. Bye."

After her death, we went about the business of the funeral. When my father pulled his suit out of the closet he brought out their wedding picture and showed me the date. My mother died one day after their 35th anniversary.

"I loved your mother very much," he said with his melting blue eyes. I hugged him and said, "I know, Papi."

I tried to make a joke as I looked at their photograph so I asked him, "So how come none of us came out as beautiful as you two?"

Still weeping, he shrugged and said, "I don't know."

Looking at the faded photograph, I could hear her telling us about the first time she fell in love with the young Spanish sergeant who could dance like Fred Astaire. His uniform was green and she wore a yellow georgette dress. Once or twice or maybe even more, I saw them dancing with my own eyes. They were so beautiful, their feet did not touch the ground.

LA MADRINA

· · · · · · · · · ·

THE GODMOTHER

OCTAVIO PAZ ONCE SAID THAT MEXICAN WOMEN HAD NO IDENTITY of their own, and that they only existed when men woke them up. Centuries before Paz, Grimm and Andersen, without ever having stepped foot in Mexico, had the same philosophy. They told us stories of sleeping princesses and damsels stuck in towers waiting to be awakened, rescued or defined by men.

As angry as it makes me to acknowledge it, I was caught in a tower, too. I pretended to be a tough cookie, all the while holding on to the husband of my childhood for dear life. I put up with the indignities of generations of Mexican women who were married to men who no longer wanted them because I did not want to be in the world without a husband. Then, bless his heart, Art did me a great service. He left. When I saw Art's back as he walked out, I took a deep breath and closed the door. Then I cried for several days and waited for the earth to open up and swallow me. Soon I expected to grow a hump and turn into a hag, as if Art, by leaving me, had taken a chunk of my femininity. I was deranged. I fantasized about how much better it would have been to save some dignity through widowhood. But after a few days, the earth felt as stable as it ever felt, my back never felt better and the birds still sang.

I came to three conclusions:

One: Of all things, my house could no longer be white. I invited everyone who loved me to paint something — the walls, the chairs, the nichos, and the chest of drawers — all in different colors. Golden corn yellow, Mexican rose, communist blue. Even the dog got an accidental streak of mango orange on his brow.

Two: For the sake of the two most important women in my life, my daughter and myself, I had to learn to live a joyful life without a man.

Three: I needed help.

The third conclusion was the most formidable. It wasn't just help in the form of support I needed, not just someone to paint a wall, provide a shoulder to cry on, break Art's legs. No, I needed a special kind of help. I needed wisdom.

The two wisest women in my life thus far had been my maternal and paternal aunts, Tía Paqui and Mamachelo. They were my *madrinas*, my godmothers. Paqui was an old maid and Mamachelo was a widow and both of them lived most of their lives without men. Perhaps I could conjure up some help from the memories they left behind.

The truth is that the presence of my Tía Paqui has never left me. I see her firmly in my past and in the current-day clutter of books, notebooks and rolls of fabric that seem to sprout out of nowhere in my house. So on that day, the first Paqui-inspired act I performed was to bake a kick-ass lemon meringue pie without a recipe, just following Paqui's instructions. The meringue healed my soul. I then went to my basket of fabric and pulled out the pieces she left me when she died. I vowed to make something out of the green and brown print. I took the fabric and put it around my shoulders like a hug. I could feel her blessings, her smiles and her kind encouragements. I remembered the best day I ever had with Paqui and was transported to a late afternoon on a mercilessly hot summer day on Rosario Street when I was 10 years old.

MADRINA № 1

· · · · · · · · · ·

TÍA PAQUI

MY PARENTS HAD TAKEN MY OLDER BROTHER AND MY BABY SISTER on another one of their trips. (The older one was too much trouble, they said, and the younger one was too young to be left, so the middle one, that one being me, got left behind.)

They left me with my grandmother and my Tía Paqui. My grandmother was mean and crazy by then and I didn't want to be there. My Tía Paqui worked all day and I was left alone to play with the servant girl, who was a couple of years older, but she had work to do. There were pigeons to catch, rabbits to pet and eggs to pick; there were errands to run and tea towels to embroider; but the long and the short of it was that until my Paqui got home from work, I was bored and restless and wanted to go home. Home, as I mentioned, had gotten into a 1959 Chevy station wagon and gone to Guaymas.

So there I was, counting the hours and the days until my family returned to pick me up and take me back to the American side of the border, where at least I had daytime television and friends to play with.

I perched myself on the corner of the garden that overlooked the street, waiting until I could see her figure coming up the hill, and then I ran to meet her to take her bags and ask her what were we going to do now. The minute my Tía Paqui got home, I would want to do something with her. I would want her to teach me how to make something, like a lemon meringue pie or biscuits, but it was too hot to turn

Francisca Moreno Gamez
"Paqui"

the oven on. Maybe today she would teach me that new stitch, the one called, "make me if you can." It was a difficult one that not too many women knew how to do.

She was tired, she said, and why didn't I come with her and take a nap in her room? But I had already taken the dreaded siesta and listened to the lizards and the pigeons count the hours. I told her I was bored. I started to cry. I wanted to go home. When was my mother coming back? Why could they take my sister and my brother on their stupid trips and not take me? Why did they leave me behind again?

She stroked my hair and comforted me but gave me no good reason except that my brother was trouble and my baby sister was still in diapers. That was not reason enough for me. Why should I be punished for being civilized?

That afternoon after her small nap, when the sun was beginning to leave its eternal center in the sky, she said to take a bath and get pretty because we were going out.

I put on the blue and pink print dress she made for me and my red rubber *calzi-plasticos*, plastic gel shoes that stuck to the hot pavement like glue if you went out in the middle of the day. But this was not the middle of the day, it was several hours past the wretched noon; the sun was beginning to move and there was a hint of rain to keep us cool. The plastic shoes made the sound of a bouncing ball against the hard dirt as we walked down Rosario hill and into town.

When I asked where we were going, she said, "You'll see. It's a surprise."

I had never been to a bookstore before. In Nogales, Arizona, we had a library but no bookstore. I liked the idea of a place where you could buy books and keep them. When I walked in, the first thing I became aware of was the distinctive aroma. I took a deep breath and it smelled like I thought heaven would smell like, cool and moist and protected from the sun. I didn't know at the time, but the musky aroma that I smelled was ink on paper, and since that day, it is one of my favorite scents. The second thing I became aware of was the jumble of books stacked on top of each other with no apparent order and no one looking over your shoulder to make sure you didn't put them in the wrong place.

My tía explained that students came here to buy their textbooks, and that you could buy comic books, *fotonovelas*, magazines, novels, cookbooks and other materials in print. There were more books there than in our small library on the American side of the border, more books than I thought could fit in such a small space. We spent what seemed like not enough time browsing and she bought me a *Pequeña Lulú* — a Little Lulu comic book — a book on cross-stitch embroidery and another on word puzzles. She also bought me a chocolate candy lollipop with caramel inside and a hard candy one shaped like a red umbrella. I was already in heaven when she took me to the corner where all the school supplies were stocked. She picked out four pencils, red, blue, green and yellow; a tiny clear green plastic pencil sharpener and a blue notebook with paper so thin, I thought it would tear if I touched it.

"Here," she said, "the next time you get bored and sad and you want to go home and you can't because there's no one there, write in this notebook."

"But what can I write?" I asked.

"You know how when you sit in the corner of the garden looking down into the street, there are many people that go by?"

I still didn't understand. She said, "Write about them. You know the washerwoman that goes by, the man that carries the table of bread on his head, the beggar that goes through the garbage foraging for food? Look inside them and make up stories. Then, write them down."

I looked at her again and she said, "That's how all these books got started, by someone writing in a notebook just like this one."

I believed her. In my imagination, the blue notebook with the onion-skin paper became a magic treasure chest of stories. I looked up and saw her gentle smile, the one that was only meant for me. I felt how much she loved me. That moment, seeing her smile and smelling a thousand books for the very first time, is permanently imprinted on my mind. I have always remembered that moment and as time goes by and it starts robbing me of my memories, I am grateful that I have written it down, right here for all time.

Did Paqui know she was changing my life by taking me to a bookstore, by telling me that all writers start their writing in a blue notebook with falling apart pages of onion skin paper? Could she have known that she was casting a spell on me that day?

Walking back home with my package in my sweaty hand, hearing the rhythm of my rubber soles hitting the hot desert dirt, the long hot summer ahead of me didn't look so grim.

We went back to Nana's house and I couldn't wait to get started. Who could I write about first? There was that old woman with the cages full of parrots on her head, the one that my grandmother said was a witch and to stay away from. I could write about her. And then there was that kid Julio who died because he talked to the pigeons and the pigeons talked back. And what about that old man, Don Nacho, who kept the store down the hill? His nose was huge! I could make up a story about why his nose grew to be gargantuan. Maybe it was because he lied like Pinocchio; maybe it was because, as my uncle Romeo said, when you get old, everything shrinks except your nose.

When my parents' dusty station wagon drove up Calle Rosario to take me back to Perkins Street, I was still yearning to get back to my American home, but I had a notebook full of stories in my bag, and three pencils, one blue, one green and one red. The yellow one had worn out.

MADRINA № 2

· · · · · · · · · ·

MAMACHELO

MAMACHELO WAS THE FIVE-MINUTE MADRINA. Everything she did, including giving me advice, she did well and in the minimum amount of time. She was a widow, wore black, and traveled. She was tall, busy, and smelled good. While my Tia Paqui was plain and fostered humility, Mamachelo was elegant and fostered arrogance. Like my mother, Mamachelo spoke with so much authority that you wouldn't even think to question that what she was saying was true. She expressed an open fondness for her own intelligence and the intelligence of others. She advised us to thank God every day because none of us were stupid.

Mamachelo came around about once a month in a whirlwind of activity with my second cousins, who were her granddaughters and so lucky because they got to go to back to Spain and visit the Louvre in Paris. I lived vicariously through their pretty clothes, what I deemed as sophisticated mannerisms, and how they came and went in the pleasantries orchestrated by Mamachelo.

Mamachelo told the stories of her childhood as if they were lessons from a book. How my grandfather was so over-protective that she wasn't allowed to go to high school, and how she went about the business of educating herself. She reported that even in her old age, she read voraciously in both Spanish and English. She read three things regularly: *Forbes* magazine for the economic news, *Time* magazine en Español, for international news, and to balance things off, *Rona Barrett's Hollywood*.

We heard about how she lifted herself out of the sadness and grief of widowhood by starting new businesses, volunteering in the community and going abroad whenever she darned well pleased. She was like a Spanish Auntie Mame without the overtones of decadence.

She had high expectations and very little use for complaints. Once when I was bemoaning some friends who were gossiping about me, she said, "Don't worry when they talk about you, dear. Worry when they don't talk about you."

She held me responsible for my actions and showered me with praise when I showed initiative or creativity.

My best day with her was when I was preparing myself for my first formal dance. My father's alcoholism was beginning to take its toll on our family, and we had fallen on hard economic times. My mother had committed to making my gown, a pale aqua blue satin that she embroidered with sequined flowers. My shoes had been dyed to match; I had borrowed a beaded purse from one of my well-to-do cousins, and all I needed were some gloves. In my mind, the gloves needed to be aqua blue but we couldn't find them in that color and to order them would have been too expensive. My mother, who had accepted a donation of a pair of long white gloves from one of her friends, insisted that white was fine, but I wanted it to be perfect. I wanted aqua blue gloves. I had read an article in *Seventeen* magazine about dying clothes, so I went to the grocery store and bought myself a couple of boxes of Ritz dye and carefully read the directions on how to create aqua blue. By some odd miracle, the gloves matched the blue of the dress to perfection. I was pleased, but not as pleased as when my

Mamachelo, who was on her monthly visit from Hermosillo, found the long gloves drying in the shower.

You would have thought I was Pablo Picasso's protégé the way she went on about how well the gloves matched the exact color of the dress. She asked me how I did it and listened to me recounting my steps. She nodded with approval and said that I had a good eye for color. Not just anyone could do this, she said. Why, she herself had created some disastrous colors. She was proud of me, she said, for taking what little resources I had to make something beautiful. She was certain that I was going to be one of most elegant girls at the dance.

Mamachelo came in and out of my life quickly and effectively. I saw her perhaps once a month when she came from Hermosillo, Sonora, to Nogales, Arizona, to shop for American products or collect her rents, but every time she came, she stopped to know me. I felt strong under her gaze.

In a long letter before she died, she told me how proud she was of me and listed all of my accomplishments, some I didn't even know she knew about.

After my divorce, I vowed to be more like Mamachelo. I made it a priority to work hard and travel with my daughter, stand up tall and smell good. I didn't spend too much time whining; it wasted time and I was busy.

They say that when you are loved right, you always go back to that love in time of crisis, so in my moments of despondency, I ran back to the memory of my two *madrinas* and I was consoled. They witnessed all my sacraments, my baptism, my confirmation and my marriage. There was only one problem. They were both dead. What I needed now was a living madrina, one that would witness the sacrament of divorce.

MADRINA № 3

· · · · · · · · · ·

DR. LEE LITTLE

MY FRIEND KAREN, WHO WAS ONE OF MY LIFELINES during my divorce, understood what I was looking for and she told me about a psychotherapist she knew. She said she grew dahlias and had hair like mine and thought we might hit it off. Dahlias are the most magnificent flowers on earth, and not too many women have hair like mine, so I called and made an appointment.

From the moment Lee gave me directions on how to find her, in a small white house in an old compound on Canyon Road, I knew that I had arrived in a place where I could find healing. Like Mamachelo and Paqui, Lee had a quick wit and a sense of humor. Her one-liners were salve to the wound.

One of the things that you can become infected with in Santa Fe is the new age philosophy that can be as helpful as annoying. I am vulnerable to these kinds of gimmicks because some of my family members were psychic, some of them were superstitious, and some of them were just plain nuts. And to this day, I don't have the discernment to tell them apart.

In my hour of need, I was pulling out all the stops. A friend of mine told me that I needed to bring good chi into my home and so recommended that I install a small pond that re-circulated water in the pathway that led to the entrance of my home. After going about the business of setting up the pond, I was to buy three goldfish and assign a good intention to each one. The three little critters were going to aid me in my journey to recovery, clean the atmosphere, and bring in good energy.

Three days later, my daughter and I came home from our long day in town and the three goldfish were floating belly-up on the re-circulating water.

All that my 16-year-old-daughter could say as she passed the catastrophe was, "Now, that can't be good."

I was devastated. Three goldfish with three good intentions dead in three days! How could this happen and what could it mean?

The next day was my first session with Lee, and I came in with my heart in my throat. I sat down and recounted that the three goldfish died in three days; I told her about the three intentions and looked at her with anticipation. She had a serene look in her eyes and didn't say a word.

"Well?" I said, eager to know what she thought. "What do you think this means?"

She shook her head softly and said, "Dear, sometimes a dead goldfish is just a dead goldfish."

I burst out laughing and I knew that I had come to the right place.

I went on to tell her that I wanted to hire Moo Gonzalez to break Art's legs. "Just save your venom for me," she said.

And that is what I did. I would go in foaming at the mouth and come out feeling cleansed. I purposefully saved my venom for Lee, as she recommended, so that I would not contaminate my daughter with my anger at her father, a decent father whom she adored. Lee's little white house was the place where I would go to separate my "stuff" so that Sara and I could grow in our separate ways. Whenever I went in worried about Sara's adolescence, Lee would say, "We know she's fine, but how are you?" And although Sara never went to Lee herself, she knew that Lee was in her corner. Whenever I got too intrusive or frantic about setting curfews or other limits, my daughter would say, "Ask Lee what she has to say about this." Sara intuitively trusted Lee to guide her distraught mother in the right direction.

Lee grew dahlias and had hair like mine. I told her once that she was the Jewish mother I never had. She smiled and called me Honey from then on. She witnessed the sacrament of my divorce, the divorce of a woman who thought she was a tough cookie until she realized that she was snagged in a tower.

Unlike Sr. Paz's archetype of the Mexican woman who only existed when men woke them up, I would point out that this Mexican woman had at least three wise women facilitate her awakening. I would also challenge Sr. Grimm and his crony Andersen and tell them that they were remiss in their recounting the stories of stranded young maidens. If they had just come in a little closer, they would have seen that it was not just the prince, the king, or the kind woodsman who saved the girl. Fairy godmothers had a hand in it, too.

LA MADRE

· · · · · · · · · ·

THE MOTHER

THERE ARE CERTAIN CONVICTIONS THAT FORM PART OF THE BACKBONE of
a family. One of ours was *La madre es sagrada* — the mother is sacred. My
mother made sure we never forgot it. She had a wholehearted belief in
her sacred status as a mother and she expected to be obeyed and vener-
ated as a result of it. But she was a Mexican mother and when it comes to
mothers, we Mexicans have it all. We have La Malinche, also known as
la chingada, the raped one, the one that sold us up the river to the Spaniards. She is the most defiled, and she still gave birth to an entire nation.
Then, on the other side of the continuum, we have the good and Blessed
Mother, la Virgen de Guadalupe, the mother of all mothers.

In Mexico, it is not uncommon for small towns and big cities to
have special monuments honoring the mother. I remember our own
Monumento de la Madre in Nogales, Sonora. It was a granite statue of a
mother and her admiring son, kneeling at her feet. There is adulation in
the boy's eyes. It's been there since the 1930's, and it still stands proudly
on Obregon Avenue. We practically genuflected when we would pass by
it on our way to buy coffee or sugar or meat at the butcher's. My mother
never failed to point it out, "Look to your left! El monumento de la
madre!" she called out proudly.

On Mexican Mother's Day, the faithful would put flowers at *la madre's*
feet. "Look at all the flowers people brought to la madre," she would say
as she careened around the corner in her powder blue 1951 Ford.

While, as Octavio Paz explains, a male macho chingón says, "Soy tu papi," to succinctly assert that you are in his domineering presence, my mother had her own version of asserting her power and I doubt she ever read Paz. "Soy tu madre," she would declare with steel in her gaze. And when she said those words, "I am your mother," and if you didn't hop-to, may God have mercy on your soul, for the depth of your regret and the appropriate penance were not too far behind.

The paradox of the power and weakness within the Mexican woman has always puzzled me. When sociologists like Oscar Lewis labeled Mexican women as submissive, I had no idea what they were talking about. In my family, you just didn't mess with women but you especially didn't mess with mothers. And when it came to our own Emmita, no matter what you did to get away from her wrath, if you violated her laws, you were pursued, found, and dealt with.

Believing that mothers were gifted with a sixth sense, she billed herself as *saurina*, which at the time I understood to mean simply psychic. Our Yaqui blood was never talked about — there were only hints of the possibility, but it wasn't until after her death that I read a book on Yaqui women where they define *saurina* as a mother who uses her psychic powers to protect her children.

The *saurina* factor always intrigued us. She could control us by simply saying, "I have a *presentimiento*." To my then teenage brother, who liked to frequent a seedy bar on the Mexican side of Nogales, she would say, "Don't go to La Nuit tonight because I have a *presentimiento*," and bam! home he was with the rest of us watching Bonanza on Sunday night. On Monday morning, my brother would find out there was a terrible fight at the nightclub and his buddy Guillermo got a black eye and spent the night in a Mexican jail. My brother, thanks to *el presentimiento de la madre*, was spared.

With all her skills and nerve, my mother was far from perfect. She was uneducated although she bragged that she repeated each grade twice, so she really got 12 years of school instead of six. She was too emotional, often violent with her words, a spoon, a shoe or whatever else happened to be at her reach. She cared too much about her looks, and subsequently yours, and had specific ideas about how the daughter she ruled was supposed to look like, act, and feel. Like Porfirio Diaz, who brought such beauty and tyranny to Mexico, she could give it and take it away. She could make you feel like a million bucks by noticing the small and significant things you did, like the time I spent my dollar allowance on an embroidered handkerchief for my grandmother. She bragged about it for weeks. I would hear her on the phone, telling my aunts, her friends, anyone who would listen. "Guess what Ana did with her allowance this week?" It made me happy to make her happy. Her approval was anointing.

But heaven help you if you crossed her, or wore the wrong outfit. "You look like the maid," she announced in the lobby as I walked down the stairs of the Hotel Laval in Hermosillo, Sonora. We had accompanied our father on one of his business trips and were spending the weekend in the capital city of Sonora. It was Sunday and we were going to church. My un-pressed yellow cotton sundress, accessorized with red rubber *chancla* flip-flops, didn't match her Kim Novak linen suit. We did not look related. She was disappointed in my choice of appropriate wardrobe for the occasion. I was 13 years old and should have known better. Her public words were a splash of water on my hot, red face.

I wish I could say that she didn't know better, but when I observed her with others she could be as gracious as Grace Kelly herself. One of her favorite explanations of how to treat people diplomatically was *con guante blanco* — with a white glove. More often than not, when she dealt in the currency of disapproval, the gloves were off.

When the gloves were off, her unleashed mother power made her a force to be reckoned with, and just as she unleashed herself on us when she disapproved, she also protected us against the world with the same unfettered passion.

All of us in the family have Emmita stories, but Lori, our youngest sister, has the most. Perhaps it was because she had the disposition of an angel and never caused anyone any harm. Perhaps it was that, with her young and tender fingers, she could cure my mother's worst migraines with her famous head massage, or perhaps it was, as we most cynically called her *lambiscona*, she was the one who sucked up to her the most. No matter the reasons or the sibling envy, Lori's reward is to have been the recipient of the most Emmita interventions. One in particular says it all.

A boy was harassing Lori at Nogales Junior High School. Lori took to wearing pants under her skirts and besides offending my mother's sense of fashion, my mother had a *presentimiento* that all was not right with her baby girl's world. When she questioned Lori about the odd habit of wearing pants under skirts, my sister wouldn't talk. Out came the bare light bulb hanging from a ceiling in the form of an Emmita statement, "Tengo un presentimiento."

It turns out there was a boy, unfortunate soul, who was flipping Lori's skirt up when she walked past him in the hallway. Lori had asked him to stop; she had told the teacher, who looked the other way and claimed Lori was exaggerating, and so the only other thing left to do was to wear pants under her skirt. At the time, girls couldn't wear pants to school; it was against the rules. Pants under the skirt, however, were apparently acceptable.

Since my mother allegedly didn't speak English (we later found out that was a lie) and the principal had been imported from some obscure town in Maine and didn't speak Spanish, Emmita took matters into her own hands.

Another one of her skills was her ability to drive anything that had wheels and drive it anyway she wanted. Parnelli Jones could not hold a candle to my mother behind the wheel of a car. She understood the meaning of car-as-lethal-weapon better than anyone. Ten years had passed since she drove her beloved 1951 Ford and she was now driving a Chevy station wagon. The gold 1963 Belair station wagon she drove was affectionately called *el buñuelo* after my father rammed it against a high wall on a narrow street in Nogales, Sonora, after one too many tequilas one fateful New Year's Eve. Nobody was hurt and in our usual way, we put a positive spin on it by christening the car after the golden sweet and deep-fried fritter traditionally eaten on December 31.

After finding out the truth about Lori's pants-under-the skirt outfit, the first thing Emmita did was drive *el buñuelo* up the hill to the school and park it right in front of the office. She waited for the boy to come out of the main building and walk across the street. She got out of the car and introduced herself as Lori's mother and told the boy that from now on Lori was going to wear skirts to school, like all the other girls. That's all she said (the *guante blanco* approach).

When Lori got in the car, Emmita explained that tomorrow she would wear her little plaid orange and brown skirt with her orange sweater and matching knee socks. It would look nice with her brown and white saddle oxfords, she said. Lori, the docile and obedient angel child she was, complied and dressed the next day in the prescribed attire.

Well, as luck would have it, the boy, not well-versed in the subtleties of Emmita's white glove communication, relished the opportunity not only to flip Lori's skirt up in front of the throng of Junior High students walking down the hallway at the end of the day, but to claim that Lori was wearing dirty underwear. Emmita was parked and patiently waiting outside the school reading the newspaper when she saw red-faced Lori run across the street to the sanctuary of *el buñuelo*.

"Let's go," Lori sobbed, slamming the door, humiliated in her orange and brown plaid skirt.

Emmita was silent and still.

"Let's go, Mami. Let's get out of here. Can't you tell what happened?"

"Just a few more minutes," Emmita said, as she waited for the boy to cross the street and unlock his bike. She started the car and waited for the boy to start riding down the steep dirt road.

"What are you doing?!" Lori exclaimed when she heard my mother rev up the engine and saw that she was following the boy down the hill.

"Don't worry," she said. "I'm not going to hurt him."

"What!" Lori recalls that Emmita's eyes had become suddenly greener. "Mami, are you crazy?"

"A little," Emmita said, "But don't worry; it's going to be okay."

"Careening" is such a wonderful word. It implies some kind of wild abandon, some kind of disregard for conventional laws.

The boy wasn't hurt, but with the skill of a race car driver fully in control of his machine, Emmita forced the boy to go over the sandy embankment of the arroyo below.

"Oh no!" Lori cried slinking down into the seat. "Oh no!" as they careened down the hill and back up again.

Emmita parked *el buñuelo* on the side of the dirt road and got out. She was wearing a green corduroy dress with a wide suede matching belt and high heels. She looked down into the arroyo where the boy was picking up his dusty bike and said, "I only give two warnings."

The boy looked up and Lori saw that he was afraid.

Rumors circulated Nogales Junior High School that Lori's mother was crazy, but my little sister never wore pants under her skirt again.

LA QUEDADA

· · · · · · · · · ·

THE OLD MAID

In Mexico in the 1960's, a woman's singular goal in life was to find a husband and have children. If, by your misfortune, you waited too long or a man didn't come along, you became an old maid, *a quedada*. That is what we called a spinster — "left behind." Another expression was to say that you missed the last bus — *el último camión*.

My Tía Paqui was in peril of missing *el último camión* when my grandfather died, leaving her in charge of the family. My oldest uncle, my mother, and my other aunt had all gotten married and started families of their own. My Tía Paqui had to take care of my grandmother, who, upon my Tata's death withdrew into old womanhood, wearing black from that day to the day she died, including a black *rebozo* she wore like a shroud, rain or shine.

Besides the widow's pension she received from the Mexican government and the adobe house my grandfather built on Rosario Street, my grandmother and the twins had Paqui. Paqui worked as secretary at the hospital in the daytime and as a teacher a couple of nights a week at the Prepa. The twins, men-of-the-house-in-waiting, weren't doing much of anything yet except eating like there was no tomorrow.

El último camión came from Hermosillo. His name was Digoberto. The day my Tía Paqui met him we were having lunch at the counter of La Campana drugstore with her friends from the hospital and he came up and introduced himself. I remember thinking he was a polite gentle-man because he stopped at our booth and said, "Buenas tardes, may I introduce myself?" and he took my tía's hand.

Digoberto was not good looking; his skin was pale and he had a thin mustache which made him look like the Boris of Bullwinkle ilk. The short double chin didn't help matters, but he had a velvety voice and when my tía stood up to walk out of the drugstore with him, he looked taller than she was, which my mother said was something of a good sign for a Mexican, since they tend to run short. My Tía Paqui was as shy as she was intelligent, but, in spite of her timidity, managed to let him take us to the movies on Sunday afternoon. The movie was *La Cucara-cha*, which my mother thought was not a movie a decent woman from a good family should see on her first date, and was not too happy about the fact that I would have to see it as well since I was the chaperone.

I was 12 years old at the time, and my Tía Paqui was 43. As a 12-year-old girl, I knew nothing about sex. I was instructed to obey my tía and close my eyes when Maria Felix, the star of the movie, dropped her bloomers. I also knew that after the movies, if I behaved myself, we would cross the border to the American side to Zula's Coffee Shop and I would get a piece of American apple pie, á la mode.

After the first date, when Digoberto dropped us off at the front porch he gave me a peso and said, "Go inside, muchacha," and I obeyed but I sneaked back up to the living room window and watched him kiss my Paqui on the lips. She smiled as she came in the front door and I scurried away. She ran after me, grabbed me, and tickled me on the bed and said, "You have to give me back that peso!" We giggled together and she asked me if I liked the apple pie and I said yes, it was *exquisito*. *Exquisito* was a new word I had learned and she always liked it when I used new words.

"Tomorrow he is taking us to the *volantines*. Would you like that?"

I squealed with happiness. My parents never took us to the carnival rides when they came to town.

"I'll finish the brown dress with the daisies for you," she said.

"What will you wear, tía?"

"I have a new beige sweater and I'll wear my black wool skirt."

"Can't you get a yellow sweater so we'll match?"

"You are such a silly girl," she said, kissing me loudly on the cheek.

"Tía, is Digoberto your boyfriend now?"

"Shush, you'll wake your Nana, now go to sleep."

We went on three dates with Digoberto. On the last date we went to dinner at the Cavern, which was the most elegant restaurant in all of Nogales, Sonora. Gringos came from all over to eat there — the food was fancy, no tacos, and there were mariachis who came to your table to sing and a photographer who took a black and white photo and put it into a white frame that said *Recuerdos de la Caverna*. We dressed up. I wore my new white dress with the brown daisies that she finished for me that day. The cap sleeves were trimmed with brown velvet ribbons. The only problem was that I only had red kneesocks.

"It's okay," she said, "just fold them down like socks. Your feet will be under the table."

"Can't you buy me white socks with lace?"

"We don't have time," she said, caring how I felt about the red socks. "I'll make you a beautiful braid and put a red ribbon in it and all the people will look at your head instead of your feet!"

She didn't wear her black skirt but a turquoise one, which was not like her at all. She wore mostly muted colors like beige and brown or black, especially since my Tata had died. She borrowed turquoise pumps and a matching purse from my mother. She had her thin black hair cut short and curled it under her chin.

I remember she looked pretty.

"Order whatever you want," Digoberto said, and so I ordered the frog legs, not because I knew what they were but because what could be better than eating frog in a new dress trimmed in velvet. After dinner they danced and I watched and his white skin turned red and I could see beads of sweat on his face as he pulled the chair out for Paqui to sit in.

On the way home, I fell asleep, but when I woke up we were parked in a dark street and they were kissing. When we got to nana's, he gave me another peso and I let myself into the house and didn't spy this time.

When she came in from kissing Digoberto, she had a gift-wrapped box and she opened it on the bed. It was a vanity set in black and white with a cameo of a lady centered on the back of the brush and mirror and in the middle of the comb.

"Look!" she said. The paper rustled and her eyes danced.

"Save the paper," I said.

"And the ribbon," she said agreeing with me. She took the brush and the mirror out and brushed her hair; she put it all back in the molded box and wrapped the paper back around as if she would want to unwrap it again, later.

She kissed me good night and said she needed to see what state the kitchen was in before going to bed. I could hear her washing dishes and putting pots away. I waited for her to come to bed so we could talk some more. I could always talk her into telling me a story about the adventures of my grandfather, who was a brave and honest man. I would wait up for her. She was my own Tía Paqui when I slept at my Nana's and I got to sleep in her big bed by the French doors and beg for a story until she gave in.

Beto, one of my teenage uncles, came home while Paqui was cleaning the kitchen and that is when they had the big fight.

"So how's your boyfriend, Paqui?" he asked, and I could tell he was mad.

"He's not my boyfriend, not yet anyway," she said calmly.

"He's never going to be your boyfriend, as far as I'm concerned."

"What's the matter with you?" Paqui said in a cross voice.

"He's a good for nothing."

"First of all Beto, that's not true, and second of all, it is really none of your business."

"First of all, Paqui, poor you, because he is a good for nothing and second of all, it is my business. This family is my business and I am not going to let anyone disgrace it."

"Beto, more respect, please," Paqui said like a big sister.

"He's a loser, Paqui."

"He's a hard-working man, Beto, and he's been kind to Ani and me."

"He's just buttering you up. I know what he wants and he better not get it. Not from you, anyway."

"You are being very vulgar and I won't have it."

"He's just going to shame you."

"There is no chance of that. Isn't that what Ani is for?"

"Thank God we have insisted that you take a chaperone."

"You insisted? Beto, you are 17 years old. I buy your underwear. You haven't earned the right to insist on anything."

"He's lying to you."

"I'm going to bed."

"I found out about him. He's married. He has a wife in Hermosillo."

"Good night, Beto," Paqui said, and I heard her walking towards the bedroom where I was pretending to sleep.

"He's a good for nothing and a liar," Beto said without altering his voice.

"Beto, if you must know, he's a journalist. He works at *The Herald* newspaper on the American side."

"He's lying to you."

"No, he's not," she said, her voice low, as she kept walking toward the bedroom.

"If he's a journalist, have you read anything that he's written? He doesn't even speak English! How can he be a journalist across the line?"

"Good night, Beto," she said as she came into the bedroom and sat on the bed. She barely made a sound when she got under the covers. I could tell by her breathing that she was awake for a long time.

The next afternoon, Paqui got out early from work and came for me and told me to put on my new street shoes. She said we were going to the American side of the line. We took the green bus to the border and crossed over. It was a short walk to the offices of *The Herald*. We went up to the front desk and Paqui asked for Digoberto Gonzalez, the journalist.

The young woman behind the desk smiled and said, "We have a Digoberto Gonzalez here, Miss, but he's not a journalist. He works the press. It is probably easier if you go through the side alley to the back of the building. You can ring the buzzer and they'll let you in."

Paqui said, "gracias," and took my hand. We walked out of the building and past the alley. I yanked her hand thinking we would go to the back of the building to find Digoberto, but she said no, that we had to hurry. If we missed the last bus, we would have to walk back and my new street shoes would give me blisters.

LA LLORONA

· · · · · · · · · ·

THE WEEPING WOMAN

UNTIL I MET MAYOYA, I always thought that La Llorona was a woman who cried too much. "Qué llorona," is what I heard about one of my tías who proclaimed that life was a valley of tears. It was Mayoya, my grandmother's "girl," who told me the story of the real La Llorona, the weeping woman who haunted the arroyos and alleys of Rosario Hill looking for her children whom, apparently, she killed.

Mayoya came to live at my Nana's house after her mother gave her away along with her five brothers and sisters. They were all of various ages, shapes, colors, and fathers and were given to different families up and down the hill. Mayoya was the eldest of what my mother called "the litter."

Mayoya's mother was a prostitute from Santa Ana, Sonora. Since she couldn't take care of her six children, she gave them away, starting at the foot of the hill across from El Mercado Tepeyac all the way up to my Nana's, and then down again to the bottom on the other side of the hill, kitty- corner to Panadería Marcelino. The family across the bakery got Ubaldo, whom Mayoya and I liked to visit. He was three years old.

Mayoya didn't talk much about her mother, but she told me all about La Llorona, who started off as a beautiful young girl with long black braids and a shapely body and ended up scaring the crap out of people at night in various places across the region. It all began, according to Mayoya, with the Cinco de Mayo parade when this handsome Charro threw La Llorona a red carnation and she picked it up. El Charro, feeling encouraged, came by La Llorona's house on his big white horse and stole her away. Men did that in those days, stole girls. La Llorona's family was a humble one without the means to chase El Charro down to make him bring her back.

After the abduction and the stolen honeymoon in Guaymas, El Charro brought La Llorona back to her folks, where she gave birth to her first baby. He then bought her a small house on one of the neighboring hills and that's where she lived, waiting for him to bring groceries. La Llorona had two beautiful children — a boy and a girl. At first, he promised to marry her, but since he was from a good family and she was not, and since he got her pregnant and set her up in a *casa chica*, he couldn't go back to his family and tell them the whole truth. That would have been a disgrace. The damage was done — La Llorona was ruined — *echada a perder*. So La Llorona cried, suffered in shame, and kept begging him to marry her and give his children his last name. El Charro resisted and said, "Ya pa qué?" What for? They had all they needed. He took care of them. She had her two fair-skinned children and one of them had blue eyes. "So, what could be better than that, Llorona?" He said. "Quit your crying and make some more tamales." (These she sold to the neighbors).

Life went on like this for a while until the day La Llorona heard the church bells ringing and the neighbors gossiping about how some rich people were getting married down at the sanctuario. The bride was going to ride sidesaddle on a big white horse. All the ladies went down to see the spectacle of two *ricachones* getting married the right way. When La Llorona got her turn at peeking through the wrought iron gates of the church she saw none other than her very own El Charro kissing the bride.

The fire that burned inside her heart consumed her. She went home and killed her children and then herself. Later on, it was El Charro with a bag of groceries who found her lying on top of her dead children.

So ever since then, according to Mayoya, La Llorona haunted the streets and alleys of Rosario hill calling out for her murdered children. "¡Ay mis niños!" she cries at night. "¡Ay mis niños!" she cries through the alleys and arroyos in the darkness.

Mayoya said that when La Llorona goes on her haunts, her face is that of a coyote, but with her same shapely body, and that it is not just children playing late in the streets that have to watch out for her, but also men who say they're working late. She beckons them to her and then devours them for being unfaithful to their wives.

So that's how I found out that La Llorona was not just a woman who cried too much.

When Mayoya told me this scary story I felt bad for her, her being given away like a kitten and all. "At least your mother didn't kill you," I said.

She glared at me and said, "Qué pinche," and went inside.

When I re-told the real story of La Llorona to my mother, she said she felt compassion. How many mothers, she said, if they were honest, wouldn't admit that they felt like killing their children for less dire circumstances than what El Charro did to La Llorona? Sure, El Charro was an *hijo de la chingada*, but what else is new? Women were used to dealing with men like that, but two kids fighting like cats and dogs? Now that was a reason to go insane. She could see how the real reason la Llorona killed her children was not that El Charro was an asshole, but because of sibling rivalry. She read about it in the Mexican magazine, *Vanidades — rivalidad entre hermanos —* the merciless bickering that robbed a mother of any pleasure she might derive from having children. Sibling rivalry was what my brother and I did; it was a form of torture and it drove my mother out of her mind. Sibling rivalry made her want to beat the crap out of us, run away and never come back. That's where those guttural warnings like, "Te voy a matar, Cabrón," came from. That's not just a warning. In case you're wondering, that's a death threat: "I am going to kill you, Cabrón."

Women can put up with bad husbands; it's bad children that make them lose their minds.

She told us about this woman she knew — La Torcuata — and she didn't kill her children like La Llorona did. She got tired of the horrible in-fighting between the little brother and the little sister, and finally left them to fend for themselves. Poor old Torcuata, *la pobrecita*, was abandoned by her husband and not unlike La Llorona, was left with her two children. Coincidentally these two children were exactly the same age as my brother and I. The brother and sister were constantly at each other's necks, bickering and fighting. One burrito was always bigger than the other. One glass of lemonade always had more than the other. According to their sibling estimates, one of them was always getting short-changed. They fought so much that La Torcuata just couldn't take it anymore. One day, she just got up from the table where the size of the tacos was being compared and debated and walked out the door. At first the children thought she had gone next door for a cup of her comadre's *café con leche* but then she didn't return for dinner.

That night the brother and sister were lonely and scared and waited for their mother to come back, but she didn't. They had enough lemonade, beans and tortillas, and the brother knew how to light a fire in the cooking stove but after a few days they began to wonder if something bad had happened to their mother or if she really had abandoned them. The brother did what he could to find food and the neighbors did what they could to help out, all the time telling the children that poor old Torcuata just couldn't take it anymore and what were they going to do now? They survived for a few more days, but on the fifth day they cried for their mother and wanted her back.

The big brother went up and down Rosario Hill asking about his mother. No one had seen her except the old washerwoman and she told him that the last time she saw La Torcuata, she was walking down the railroad tracks with a blank expression on her face, mumbling nonsense. So the boy went back home and told his sister to put on a *rebozo* because it was cold. They were going to go look for their mother. The two children set out to find La Torcuata, who by now might have gotten all the way to Imuris. So they walked down the railroad tracks. They walked past the statue of *El Mono Bichi*, the Naked Man. He was still killing the dragon. They walked past the railroad station on the outskirts of town. They walked all the way to where they could see only hills and nothing but mesquite trees for miles and miles. They miscalculated the amount of daylight they had and it got dark and cold. Over by a pile of garbage and wood, they ran into an old beggar who yelled at them and told them to go home and what were they doing out there alone on a dark cold winter night. He waved his dirty hand at them and said it was a good thing he didn't like children or else he would eat them for dinner. The big brother grabbed his little sister's hand and ran down the tracks until they came to an old mesquite tree with a wide hollow trunk. The wind was getting colder and they huddled together and wept and the boy asked for his sister's forgiveness for all the times he had cheated her out of her lemonade when she wasn't looking and the girl said she was sorry for breaking his model airplane on purpose. The brother held his sister to his chest and said, "Don't worry *Manita*, I'll take care of you," and that's how they fell asleep.

Just about when the cold was so unbearable they thought they would freeze, the gray light of morning came, but the wind was howling even more and they weren't comforted by the promise of the sun. That's when they both heard the cry. It sounded like a coyote, the way it can imitate a woman screaming. The boy thought the wailing was the devil himself coming to claim him for being so bad and he thought the only thing to do was run. He grabbed his sister and got back on the railroad tracks. Maybe the early train from Imuris would come and stop and help them. The howling was getting closer and the boy thought he heard "¡Mis niños! — ¡Ay mis niños!"

The girl stopped and said, "Wait, it sounds like Mami."

But the boy said it was the devil's trick and if they stopped he would devour them. He told his sister to pray the Hail Mary very loud to drown out the wailing that was catching up to them. The little sister yelled out the prayer as hard and fast as she could as they kept running. And then, she heard the voice call out her name. The brother stopped and looked at his sister. Then he heard his name being called as clear as the cloudless sky that was being lit up by the sun rising over the barren hills.

When they both looked behind them, expecting to be devoured by the wild animal that the devil had become, they saw that it was La Torcuata. She threw herself on her knees and gathered them up in her arms and begged for their forgiveness.

"I've been a bad mother," she cried. "Please forgive me."

They were so happy to see her that they showered her with a million kisses and I'm sorries and she rocked them back and forth against her soft body and murmured, "Ay mis niños. Ay mis niños."

After that day, according to my mother, the brother and sister didn't misbehave again and from that moment on they called each other *manito* and *manita*. And they walked hand in hand to do their errands and never complained nor compared the sizes of their bean burritos or scoops of ice cream.

LA CRIADA

. . . .

THE MAID

WHEN I WAS GROWING UP IN NOGALES, ARIZONA, I did nothing around the house except wash my own underclothes — panties, slips, camisoles, and pajamas. I washed them by hand because my mother said they would get ruined in the old roller machine. My mother did the cooking and the rest of the wash.

The maid did everything else — *la muchacha* is what my mother called her, "the girl." We had several girls throughout the years. My mother called the maids, muchachas; others called them *criadas*, a term my mother frowned upon and one we weren't allowed to use; and still others called them *gatas* — implying that they were stray cats and could be treated as such. My mother never had to admonish us about the use of the term *gata*. I had never been too fond of cats and to call a girl a *gata* made me feel like I had to go to confession. Some people made their girls wear uniforms, another custom my mother disapproved of. Not only was it cruel to make someone who earned so little money wear a uniform, she said, it was also pretentious in our middle class house of only three bedrooms.

Being a *muchacha*, especially if you were young, had its advantages, mostly economic. Poor Mexican families from rural villages and ranches would send their daughters to the border cities to work for middle and upper class families and it was a quasi-respectable thing to do for a living. It was better than staying in the village and suffering from hunger, and it was certainly better than taking the wrong road and ending up a prostitute. It was a way for these girls to work, send money home, and stay out of harm's way. The biggest risk the girls took was being sexually exploited by unscrupulous *patrones*. My father was a man of honor in that regard. Besides the fact that he worked most of the time in Mexico and wasn't home much, his bad habits were tightly contained inside a bottle of tequila, so our home was safe.

For as long as I could remember, we had a *muchacha*. They came to us with their meager possessions: an extra change of clothes, a small bag of sundries. They slept in a foldout cot in our bedroom and were given one drawer to put their things in. They stayed all week, leaving on Sunday and returning on Monday morning when my mother would pick them up at the border crossing. The girls came and went; some lasted a few days, some a few months, and if it worked out, they lasted years.

There was Panchita, who had to get fired because she once flirted with my father and what kind of foolishness was that? Back to Caborca she went. There was Ramona, who was so fat and loved to eat so much that my mother had to hide the food to no avail because Ramona was such a thorough housekeeper that she found all the hidden goodies and ate them anyway. There was Natalia, who looked like Jackie Kennedy and managed to dress like her too — and how she did that on 10 dollars a week was beyond explanation until we read about her arrest one Monday morning when she didn't show up at the border crossing for my mother to pick her up. Apparently, selling heroin was a much more lucrative endeavor than being a *muchacha*.

Some of these girls that came and went weren't girls. They were older — women who had to support the children they left behind in their villages, or homeless women who hadn't married or had no family and needed a way to live a decent, if impoverished, life.

In spite of the fact that it was cheap to have a *muchacha* and great to live in a spotless house, it wasn't always easy. One time we had this older woman, Rosenda, from Magdalena, Sonora, and you could tell she felt uneasy with the arrangement. She liked to read books and after she ate her dinner, which was always after we ate dinner, and after she cleaned the kitchen for the night, she would ask my mother if she could sit in the living room and read since she didn't like to watch television. You could tell my mother wasn't crazy about the idea of Rosenda sitting in the living room. The living room was the special room where none of us were allowed to go. It was for other people, such as guests and not for us, and it was certainly not for the help. It had the good velvet sofa and the glass cabinet with all the crystal stuff and the Lladró figurines of Don Quixote and Sancho Panza. It was off-limits, but my mother didn't say no when Rosenda asked if she could read in there after her work was done. My mother said yes. She explained to us that Rosenda wasn't like the other *muchachas*; she was older and had been a schoolteacher; she had fallen on bad times so she was working as a maid to make ends meet.

It happened one day that my mother made chicken in mole poblano for dinner. As usual, we ate dinner before Rosenda. And we all said how delicious the mole was and my mother even said that it was the best mole she had ever made. We got carried away and by the time Rosenda sat down to dinner, all that was left of the chicken in mole poblano was a pile of bones in the pot. It was cold that night and it must have been December because my mother had gone up to the attic and pulled down the plastic elf she always placed on the rooftop before Christmas.

My mother tried to be nice and said, "Rosenda, I am so embarrassed. The kids and I ate all the chicken and all that is left is the mole sauce. There's beans and rice, but all the chicken is gone. I'm sorry."

Rosenda went up to the stove and peered inside the large pot with the bones in mole sauce and she took the blue enamel spoon that was lodged inside the pot and hit the stove with it and screamed, "The time of slavery is over!" She kept hitting the stove with the spoon and repeating this over and over again.

Well, no maid, young or old, had every screamed at my mother and it was clear that my mother didn't know what to do. She stammered, "Please, Rosenda, we didn't do it on purpose. The sauce is so dark, I couldn't really see that the meat was gone," and she tried to explain and Rosenda got the large enamel spoon and threw it across the kitchen, at which point my mother said it was time for us to go to bed, which was odd because there was no such thing as bedtime at our house; you went to bed when you were tired and that was it. But we all scurried out of the kitchen and my mother followed us into the television room. When the Lawrence Welk show was over, we heard the front door that led to the outside from the living room close, and my mother looked at us in the dark room and said, "She's gone." We never saw Rosenda again.

Then came Yoli. She was our best girl. She came to us when she was 13 years old and I was 10. Yoli was from Michoacán and had eight brothers and sisters and white skin. She slept on the cot in our bedroom and didn't seem to mind.

At night, we ate dinner first, and then she ate and washed the dishes. At bedtime with the lights out, she would tell us stories of her family in Uruapan, and how their father left one day to go to work in the United States and never came back, and how her mother Berta brought them to Nogales to see if they could find him. Yoli was the oldest of the family and helped her mother support her younger brothers and sisters; she had a sweetness about her and was so polite that we learned our best manners from her.

Her best talent, besides making killer flour tortillas, was that she could tell a mean story in the dark. She told us stories of her village and how they used to put on variety shows and make their own costumes out of crepe paper. Once she told us a story about a pretty girl with big hips who went to work as a maid in the city and got fired and became a prostitute and worked on Canal Street in a red dress. Another time she told us about an evil man in her village who liked to scare little kids for sport and how the men in the village got together and beat him up and would have killed him if the priest hadn't intervened at the last minute.

We got to be pretty close and Yoli became like our sister. She started calling us *manito* and *manita* — little brother and little sister. She was very affectionate and would kiss my baby sister and me good-night. My brother, who was older than Yoli, didn't get a kiss and he would tease her and ask, "Hey Yolanda, don't I get a kiss?"

And she would say, "No, señorito, you certainly don't!"

He would laugh at her and she would try to hide her smile and ignore him.

Yoli started going to mass with us on Sunday mornings and my mother bought her black patent leather Mary Janes like mine and gave her a red plaid dress that was too big for me and she became part of our family. Once in a while, Yoli would be mistaken for a real sister, and at mass one day a lady said to my mother, "Emma, I didn't know you had an older daughter!" My mother smiled and said, "You didn't?" And when we walked away, we all had a good laugh.

One night after the tenth repeat performance of the story about the mean man who got beaten to a pulp in her village, I asked her, "Yoli, why do you always eat dinner after we do?" I felt bad asking her because after the Rosenda experience, I had a pretty good idea but I asked anyway, and she said, "Because you and I are not the same."

It was dark in our bedroom when she said that and she didn't say anything else so I went to sleep feeling bad about asking such a question. The next evening at dinner while Yoli heated up tortillas and we ate our *papas con chorizo*, I asked my mother point blank: "Why can't Yoli eat with us instead of by herself?"

My mother looked at me with those giant hazel eyes of hers and didn't answer. My brother, who was older and had a more sarcastic way of being since he was nearly 15, said, "Maybe it's because we're better than she is," and he filled his mouth full with this huge tortilla and his cheeks looked like they were about to explode and he arched his eyebrows, teasing Yoli.

My mother gave him a look that could have melted him into a puddle of ooze under the table. "Yoli can eat with us," my mother said, still giving my brother the evil eye. She went up to Yoli and kissed her on the head like she always did me and said, "Sit down, hija," and Yoli sat down with us at the round kitchen table and my mother served her *papas con chorizo* before she served herself.

It got real quiet and my brother said, "Amá these are the best *papas con chorizo* you ever made!"

My mother glared at him again and he glared back and then we all started laughing. Yoli stayed with us for four more years, until she was 17 and met a young man who worked at the post office on the Mexican side of the line. When she got married, we all went to her house for wedding cake.

Yoli was our best girl.

LA BEATA

· · · · · · · · · ·

THE WOMAN
IN THE SERVICE OF GOD

I WOULD SEE THEM SOMETIMES after the crowds left the church or when we came too early to mass — these wrinkle-faced ladies in black, cleaning the altars and sweeping the church. To me they looked like widows, mourners with their heads covered in tight black scarves, their feet wrapped up in rope-soled *alpargatas*, mumbling as they swept. My Nana said they were *beatas*, women in the service of God, and that their mumbles were prayers. When I asked if it was like being God's maid, she said yes, but that I shouldn't feel too much pity. They would get their rewards in paradise. But try as I might to see *las beatas* singing and dancing it up in heaven, all I saw were grouchy old ladies hunched over their brooms.

If it was a heavenly honor to clean up after the Father, the Son and the Holy Ghost, it didn't look all that enjoyable to me. Better, I thought, to be a nun. There were some pretty ones, like my catechism teacher, Sister Celeste. She had blue eyes and she did look like the bride of Jesus and I could see why Jesus would want to marry her. Jesus and Sister Celeste would make a good couple and if it weren't against the rules they could have cute children, but I stopped with those thoughts because Zonia Ahumada told me that nuns married Jesus but they could never have children because part of being the bride of

Christ was to have your boobs amputated. That's why the sisters were so flat-chested, she said, because they had to have an operation. But still, nuns were better off, I thought, than those poor old ladies wearing black, frowning while they dressed the saints.

Being a *beata* was one of those things you could be if:

    a.) You couldn't find a boy to marry you.

    b.) You got married but your husband died.

    c.) Time ran out and you missed the chance to be a nun.

    d.) Your husband left you for a racecar driver.

D is what happened to my Tía Gloria. My Tío Roberto, who I liked a lot because he looked like the cowboy on the telenovela we were watching, left her over and over again for different women and then finally, the last time, he left her for a racecar driver. That's when the Holy Ghost appeared to my tía and inspired her to become a *beata*.

I heard all this when they thought I was napping. It was the last straw, they said. He was a *sin vergüenza*, a man without shame, a typical *bronco*. He never appreciated my tía and he got all *alborotado* — excited with this racecar driver because there weren't that many Mexican women who raced cars for money, and how could my Tía Gloria compete against that?

I imagined that my tía was left in a big cloud of dust and the racecar driver lady and my cowboy uncle peeled out and left my Tía Gloria standing there with her four children. That's when the white pigeon appeared in the sky — *el espiritu santo*. I could see how it all happened. Upon turning away from the cloud of dust, she had tears in her eyes and she looked up to heaven for strength and there the bird was hovering over her head, white against the blue Sonoran sky. That's when she threw herself on her knees and prayed that the Holy Ghost take her to Jesus.

When my aunt and mom said that Tía Gloria had decided to serve God and become a *beata*, somehow I couldn't see my aunt dressed in black wearing funky shoes. One of the things I loved about her, besides her spiked heels, was the brightly colored skirts she wore cinched with a wide belt around her skinny little waist. She had these hips that swayed when she walked and legs that made men howl when she crossed the street. It was hard for me to imagine my Tía Gloria as a *beata* wearing black, hunched over a broom. It sure as hell would take a long time for her to shrivel up like a raisin and look like a beata, but regardless of what I thought, my tía surrendered herself to the service of God.

It took a while for us to get used to the idea, and although she gained weight and lost her skinny little waist, she continued to dress in brightly colored dresses and took to wearing a turban. In between gaining weight and taking to wearing a turban she discovered that she was psychic so she became somewhat of a mystic maid to the Holy Trinity and started laying hands on those who needed healing. My mother said she took a bad situation and made it good, made it fit to what she needed to be a happy woman without a man.

As I grew into my teenage years I came to see her as a hybrid between Mark Twain and Aretha Franklin. She gave out free advice and had a quip for everything. She could sing a mean *alabanza* — those ancient Spanish spiritual songs that made Indians convert to Catholicism and gave you goose bumps. When she sang, you stopped to listen. This was the Holy Ghost, she said, that made her do that. Everything she did she credited to the Holy Ghost. From a kick-ass *menudo* to a clothes drive for the poor; it was all the work of the Holy Ghost. If she was God's servant, she was also his stand-up comic because when she told a joke, you laughed until you cried and almost peed in your pants.

When we were possessed by this joyful laughter she would remind us that the Holy Ghost had a sense of humor.

At my beloved Tía Paqui's funeral when my Tía Gloria broke out in song and I felt the surge of joy replace the sadness, I knew that if there was such a force as the Holy Ghost, my tía Gloria had found it. It was at the funeral that I finally understood that a woman, in addition to being in the service of a husband, in the service of her children, in the service of her aging mother when no man would have her, could also be in the service of God. It was a more viable option than marrying Jesus and having your boobs amputated.

My tía Gloria gave up on mortal men and turned to the Father, the Son, and the Holy Ghost when she was left in a cloud of dust by my cowboy uncle who preferred a racecar driver. Instead of shriveling up like an old crone, to our surprise, she was filled with joy.

Now that I am over 50, and I am like those women I considered old and kooky when I was watching their every move, I understand that my Tía Gloria in her surrender to God was wilder in her devotion than anything she could muster up for her husband and that with the Holy Ghost, she suffered less.

LA VIUDA

· · · · · · · · · ·

THE WIDOW

ON THE KITCHEN TABLE OF OUR FAMILY HOME in Nogales, Arizona, was a permanent centerpiece: a bottle of tequila with a picture of a beautiful white-skinned woman wearing a black lace mantilla — La Viuda de Martinez. I would sit and stare at the picture of the widow on the bottle because it made me think of Mamachelo, my father's oldest sister and the matriarch of the family.

Mamachelo had been left a widow when my Uncle Salvador died of a heart attack. She was 45 years old when he died and I don't remember much about my uncle except that he worked at the bank, came home for lunch every day, and had a kind deep voice. What I do remember in vivid detail was Mamachelo and the house by the cathedral in Guaymas, Sonora. The house was Mamachelo personified: expansive, interesting, and always busy.

Once after my uncle's death, when she was still wearing black, I saw Mamachelo sign a document that they brought over from the bank. She wrote "Consuelo Matiella, Viuda de Martinez." Her new status as "the Widow of Martinez" was so present in her life that it was affirmed every time she signed her name. When I saw "Viuda de Martinez" on the line she signed at the bottom of the paper, I thought about the beautiful lady on my father's tequila bottle and how she, too, had the dignified and wise look that Mamachelo wore with such confidence.

They say she never wanted to marry again and as a child, I wondered why. Why would this beautiful, regal, intelligent woman with so much love to give not want to marry again? So I asked my mother, who was married to a man who loved tequila more than he loved her, and she said, "Why should she want to get married again? Look at all she has." My uncle had left her some money, but she also ran two businesses of her own, a restaurant and a curio shop she called, what else, but "Consuelo's?" My mother went on with admiration and envy and said, "She doesn't need anything but what she has. She can devote herself to her businesses and her grandchildren; she has perfected the art of being a *dueña* to her granddaughters when being a *dueña* is a dying art." But most importantly, my mother said, "she has her freedom. And why would she ever want to give that up?"

From my mother's perspective, being the widow of an honorable man was about the best status you could have in Mexico. Seniority, respect, position, suffering, and overcoming loss, were highly valued accomplishments for a woman in Mexican society. "No," my mother said, "she would be foolish to marry again." Still curious and not satisfied with my mother's account of Mamachelo's voluntary singlehood, I approached her myself when I was about 15 years old, "Mamachelo, would you like to get married again?" And she said, "No, dear, I like to travel alone."

Although it was an odd response, I came to realize much later that it was widowhood that enabled my aunt to live as an independent woman. And it wasn't that she didn't consider what it might be like to have another lifetime companion, or that she didn't have prospects. My mother was fond of retelling the story about the admiral.

There was this retired gringo admiral living in Guaymas at the time and socializing in the same circles as Mamachelo. He escorted her to several functions, such as Lion's Club dinners and orphanage inaugurations, and apparently fell in love with her. When he asked her to marry him, she was flattered. Here was a good and honorable man and if she were going to consider remarrying, he would have been suitable. But as the story was told, in the same breath of — "Will you marry me?" — he also declared passionately that he was tired of being alone, not getting any younger, and eventually would need someone to take care of him.

She politely declined the offer.

My mother told me that later when they had a chuckle about the proposal, Mamachelo said, "Now why would I want someone else to take care of, Emma? Is it not enough that I already take care of my aging mother, chaperone my granddaughters and take care of two businesses?" No, she didn't need to "take care" of the Admiral, no matter how suitable he was. She was a widow, Viuda de Martinez. A widow had respect, a protected place next to an honorable dead man's memory, and the freedom to travel alone.

★

When my husband of 25 years left, I was grief-stricken and felt amputated. Shopping one day for no particular reason except to ignore the hole that I felt inside, I went to my favorite Mexican folk art store. Ever since Mamachelo had her curio shop, I have always found comfort among clay figurines and embroidered tablecloths. I came across a clay figurine by one of the Aguilar sisters from Oaxaca. It was of a man lying in a coffin, with his hands folded over his chest. A woman, presumably his bereaved wife, lay her head over him and wept. He was dead; she was a widow; I was envious.

"How much better would it have been," I reasoned, "if Art had simply died." I stood there mesmerized by the widow and her dead husband and fantasized. Art had life insurance and I would have been the beneficiary. For half a million dollars I could pull my daughter out of school, homeschool her myself, buy fabulous black clothing, and travel around the world as in a Henry James novel. The widow Naegelin and her budding beauty of a daughter — what adventures we could have had! In my mind's eye there was a rustic but gorgeous villa in Tuscany with a servant named Enzo. And how about that cute little bungalow on the beach in Andalucía? At the end of our stay at each of these fabulous places, I would sign my name: Ana Consuelo Matiella, Viuda de Naegelin. Then off we would rush with our steamer trunks to a car waiting that would take us to the next cruise ship.

We would lick our wounds, in style, on the Mediterranean. We would write post cards from exotic places. We would remember how funny my poor departed husband was, or how charming he was, or the time he lost his temper because the lines to the ferry were too long. And I would tell my daughter about the first time we went to a formal dance, and what I wore, and the first time he told me he loved me, and all the pet names he had for her when she was a baby, and how good he was at changing diapers. And all the anger and resentment of the years of broken promises would boil down to the essence of a good husband. Death eventually heals all wounds.

When I came out of my fantasy, I was still standing there looking at the figurine of the widow and her dead husband. I bought it. I took it home, laid it on the table, and lit two candles, one on each side. I then called my travel agent and booked us a trip to Spain. It was too hot for black in Spain in the summer so I bought white linen instead.

LA QUERIDA

• • • • • • • • • •

THE MISTRESS

DOÑA CLARA MOVED OUT OF HER MINT GREEN HOUSE on Rosario
Street one somber Sunday afternoon while all the neighbors watched
through the cracks in the curtains. She had lived on top of the rocky
hill for 20 years. I didn't know much about the mysterious lady who
lived in the well-kept house, but what I did know I learned from
over-hearing my grandmother's conversations with Doña Pelona, the
neighborhood busybody. *Metichi* is what they called her — this Doña
Pelona. She sold and delivered cheese and eggs in the neighborhood
and brought my grandmother discarded issues of *Doctora Corazón*.

Doctora Corazón was an illustrated historieta, a graphic novel in se-
pia tones, depicting true stories and tragic tales of morality and love. If
Dear Abby had been Mexican and creative, she would have published a
similar publication. Dejected lovers and victims of tragedy would send
their stories to *Doctora Corazón*, and she, doctor of the heart, would put
the psychodrama into pictures and give desperately sought out advice.
The story was often told in the first person and would end with a frantic plea for help, "*¡Ayúdeme, Doctora Corazón!*"

Doña Clara kept to herself and to the garden she tended in front of
her mint green house. She looked like an upgraded version of the rest
of the old ladies on Rosario Street. She had all her teeth and her shiny
black hair was combed back in a braided bun; she wore well-pressed
and starched aprons with appliquéd embroidered flowers.

On any given morning when we walked past her house, you could see her wearing a different colored apron, washing down the shiny red cement walkway that divided her garden into two equal parts. Besides the roses, daisies, and dahlias that grew in the garden, the whitewashed porch had a wide array of colorful geraniums, coleus, and Angel Wing begonias. Her parakeets and canaries hung there in cages painted different colors, and there was one large, green, and noisy parrot that squawked and serenaded the neighbors with Agustín Lara songs.

Doña Clara's house was an inviting place, yet we never crossed its ornate white iron gate. The flowers begged to be smelled or cut or made into crowns; the parrot was so charming, what would be wrong with us coming to visit and bringing him a mango? Sometimes I liked to imagine that Doña Clara's house was like the witch's house in "Hansel and Gretel," and that something bad would happen if you broke through its enticing beauty. It wasn't that Doña Clara was unfriendly or scornful, but it was clear she preferred to be left alone. The beautifully-kept mint green house with the white front porch was off- limits, a cool oasis in the dusty, noisy and rambunctious hill that was Rosario Street.

Coming up the hill from buying sugar or flour at the corner store, I would notice certain things about Doña Clara and her life in the pretty green house. Although she lived alone, she had a Yaqui girl come in to help her every day. The girl was young, about 13 or 14, and she never spoke to us even when we crossed paths on our daily errand runs. She kept to herself even more than Doña Clara, because at least Doña Clara would smile at us once in a while. Another thing about Doña Clara was that she had a weekly visit from an old man in a black chauffeured Lincoln Continental. The chauffeur slept in the car parked in front of the garden gate with his hat over his eyes, while Doña Clara and the old man sat on the front porch and had coffee with sweet bread. Sometimes the old man wore a dark green uniform with gold epaulettes; other times he just came in a regular suit and tie. He never went inside that we could tell and he didn't stay long. He just had his café con leche and left.

My grandmother referred to her as Doña Clara, as did the rest of the ladies in the neighborhood, but Doña Pelona, the egg and cheese lady, called Doña Clara, *la mujer del comandante*, the *comandante's* woman. From eavesdropping on my grandmother's and Doña Pelona's weekly business and gossip transactions, I learned that Doña Clara was the old man's mistress and that she had once been beautiful. "And what a pity it was," my grandmother said, "that she never married properly because she came from good families." It was easy to see that Doña Clara had once been a beautiful girl because to me she was a very pretty lady, all clean and shiny, but what I didn't understand in my child's mind was how she and *El comandante* could have sex on the porch. All they did as far as I could tell was talk softly, drink café con leche and eat sweet bread.

My grandmother was a recluse; the world came to her. The vegetable man came to deliver the vegetables; the bread man passed by with a table of hot and fragrant bread on top of his head; the tortillera came and made tortillas in the yard on the grill that my uncle made out of a steel oil drum. We ran the errands; my aunt went to the butcher's, and Doña Pelona came once a week to deliver more than eggs and cheese.

On one of her delivery days, I heard Doña Pelona say, "Why does he come to visit her still? He's so old." And then she cackled, "he can't be good for much anymore."

"Who are we to judge?" my grandmother said after hearing Doña Pelona's latest report on the life of Doña Clara.

Doña Pelona and my grandmother had known each other for years and although my grandmother called Doña Pelona a *mitotera*, she always had hot coffee ready when Doña Pelona made her weekly deliveries.

From Doña Pelona I heard that a long time ago, Doña Clara had given birth to a baby boy and that she gave the baby to her sister to raise in Empalme. "And then off he went to boarding schools to study in San Diego, California. No one has seen him around Nogales, but his name is Efraín, " she said.

"Who are we to judge?" my grandmother said as she poured more thick *café con leche* into Doña Pelona's cup.

"I'm not judging her, Concha," she said, "it's just that she thinks she's so *popof*! She's no better than any of us, really. In all the years that we have lived in this barrio, has she ever given you the time of day?"

"She likes to keep to herself, but she harms no one, Pelona. Tell me, what harm does she do?"

Doña Pelona was more agitated that day than usual. "Do you know that she has never bought not even one miserable egg from me?"

My grandmother poured more coffee.

"She gets her provisions delivered by that silly man in the chauffeur's uniform!" Doña Pelona gulped her coffee down and kept talking. "Well sooner or later, the truth comes out!" Doña Pelona wiped the sugar crumbs off her toothless mouth with the back of her arm. "The truth comes out."

She reached down into her mercado bag and pulled out two tattered issues of *Doctora Corazón* and slapped them on the table. "Here, Concha, so you won't get bored before my next visit. They aren't that good, really. My stories are so much better!" She laughed out loud as she took my grandmother's pesos and stuck them in her worn-out apron pocket.

Later, I saw the graphic novels on the table. One was about a wife who found out that her husband was having an affair with the maid.

The other was about an aging mother who was being mistreated by her adult daughter. Both sad stories of actual people, some as far away as the capital and some as close as nearby Magdalena, Sonora.

On another of Doña Pelona's weekly visits, she was irate because Doña Clara's Indian girl told her to go away when she opened the garden gate and tried to come in with a basket full of her best eggs. "Now you know I go and come as I please in this neighborhood!" she shrieked, "That Indian has some nerve! Just like her uppity *patrona*. What do you expect?"

"But God works in mysterious ways, no? As it turns out I heard that the *comandante's* legitimate wife has cancer and she's not going to be around that long," she went on. "They say he might finally marry Clara! Ha! At this age? How ridiculous! Do you think she'll wear a wedding gown?" Doña Pelona's cackles pierced my ears.

My grandmother said to Doña Pelona, "I've lived here for 40 years and all I know about Clara is what you've you told me. She is a very private woman. How do you know all these things?"

"You would be surprised," she said, "how much I know, how much I've learned from 40 years of selling eggs." She put two more teaspoons of sugar in her coffee. "Why the stories I could send to *Doctora Corazón!*"

The reason they called her *La Pelona* was that she had no hair and wrapped her head in a scarf. As far as I was concerned they could call her *La Molacha*, too, because she had no teeth.

My grandmother didn't find out what happened to Doña Clara from Doña Pelona. She found out because I told her that when I passed by on my way to buy coffee I saw they were taking the big parrot's covered cage into the large black car and all the plants were out in front of the gate. My grandmother didn't like to get out that much, but she asked me to go up the hill with her. There was a group of women murmuring across the street and I went and stood there with my grandmother. One of the ladies had the latest copy of *Doctora Corazón*, and I could tell the story was about Doña Clara because the first illustration was of the big black Lincoln Continental parked in front of the gate. In one of the frames, a young man in uniform walked up the garden walkway. He was carrying a bouquet of flowers. A young Doña Clara waited in the threshold of her porch, smiling. In the corner of the frame, in an oval, was a woman weeping with her face in her hands. The headlines read *"¡La mujer del comandante!"* And then, the customary splashy title across the page: *"¡Ayúdame, Doctora Corazón!"*

The story was told in lurid detail: the part about the comandante's 40-year affair with Clara, the indignities that the legitimate wife and children suffered, all about Clara's bastard son who lived in Phoenix, and the shame that kept him from visiting his mother. The story was written from the *comandante's* wife's point of view, from her deathbed.

I helped my grandmother back down the steep hill and when we passed Doña Pelona's, my grandmother glared at her and mumbled something to herself. Later, after the mint green house had been boarded up and was taken over by the dust that plagued the rest of the neighborhood, I heard my aunt, who worked at the hospital where the *comandante's* wife had been treated, tell my mother and grandmother that it wasn't true that the *comandante's* dying wife had sent in the story to *Doctora Corazón*. She had learned about the story because someone had left a copy of the graphic novel on her hospital bed while she slept.

After that, when Doña Pelona came to the house to sell eggs and cheese, my grandmother wouldn't open the door. She just peered out through a crack in the curtain and watched Doña Pelona knock, louder and louder until she gave up and went on her way.

LA SUEGRA

• • • • • • • • • •

THE MOTHER-IN-LAW

OUR CHILDREN ALWAYS COME FIRST. We have been known to abdicate our roles as wives and trade them in for mothers. I have a friend who is a widow and she told me, "Honey, you and I know that husbands come and go, but our children are ours forever … " Her husband died and mine up and left and so I agreed with her. But even with death and divorce aside, I come from a place that has little faith in the permanence of men. My father, as far as I know, was faithful to my mother, but he had another mistress and that was his beloved bottle of tequila. Although he provided for us financially, in my mother's eyes, he was not that dependable. My former father-in-law told me once, and picture that it was at my mother-in-law's funeral, about his wives. "Wives," is what he said and "wives" is what he had. He never bothered to hide it: he had wives, and he had families. Two of each, that we knew of.

So is it any wonder then that our children always come first? In the world that I have lived in, our husbands are much more likely to leave us than our children are. If we play our cards right, our children will never leave us, not in the true sense of the word. I mean, they may move to Washington, D.C., or Barcelona, or Portland, but they will not leave us, not where it counts, not in the heart. In their hearts, we are their beloved mothers. Besides not leaving us, they are even less likely to betray us. Like with chicken pox or whooping cough, we know how to inoculate them against abandoning and betraying us. When it comes to children, if we are worth our salt, we Mexican mothers know what we're doing.

Now having a daughter is a blessing beyond belief, and if she is good and kind, likes to shop, and has a sense of humor, there is no end to the joy that she will enrich our lives with. In the best-case scenario, she will bless us with grandchildren. Then, we will know the true meaning of who-needs-men-anyway.

But as wonderful as it is to have a daughter, having a son is the ultimate reward. Having a son is like having a good insurance policy — we're in good hands. Of course, it is better to have both a son and a daughter. That is the best situation, one of each. But face it, our sons can do for us what our daughters cannot. For one thing they can recognize, man to woman, what we sacrificed and what we suffered. For another, they can give us male attention without all those other in-conveniences. And finally, if we are very good and very lucky, they will actually understand that the mother is sacred. Some people say that mother-veneration is a Mexican thing and I think they're right. You might call it stereotyping, but tell me quick how many songs you have heard from non-Mexican men about their mothers? None. Now, listen to a few mariachis or boleros or tangos and you won't have to wait too long before you hear the likes of Pedro Infante, Jorge Negrete, or Cuco Sanchez weeping into the microphone about his *madrecita*. "In a little house, very pretty, very white … " You know the one. The be-nevolent mother waving from the window of her *casita blanca*.

I came from a world where children always came first, where if you could choose between having a son and having a daughter, you would choose a son, and where if you had to choose between your husband and your son, you would still choose your son. If you don't believe me, ask any Mexican woman if her husband was drowning and her son was drowning who she would save, and there you'll have it.

So the power of *La Madre* is strong and everlasting and having a son is about the best thing you can do for yourself. But if you are the wife, I don't need to tell you that the mother-in-law, *La Suegra*, is a force to be reckoned with. I learned this lesson when I was seventeen on a visit to Tijuana, Baja California at a bridal shower. I learned that having a good *suegra* is just plain good luck — good karma, as the gringos say, but having a bad *suegra* is like being stuck in a hornet's nest.

I had a *suegra* once and she was nothing like the *suegras* at the Tijuana bridal shower or even like the ones we see on the telenovelas. I had good *suegra* karma. Julia, my first husband's mother, was kind to a fault. This is exactly what people would say about her: "She was so good, she was good for nothing." The women in Nogales said that she would go to heaven with her *guaraches* on, meaning that when she showed up at the pearly gates, she would not have to remove her shoes like everybody else. I could see that if anyone could go to heaven with her *guaraches* on, it would be Julia. *Abnegada*, is what people called her. I looked up *abnegada* in the Spanish dictionary. It means to deny one's self, and deny herself she did. She never put herself first — she was always last and with so many children and a husband who thought he was Zorba the Greek in a Charro suit, she was at the tail end of a long line. The other adjective used to describe her was *sufrida*. That means she suffered so much, she became the suffering. Now if you know about Mexicans you know these are the qualities of a *santa mujer*, a saintly woman, and they said that too. "She was a saint." That is why Julia had to wait to get to heaven before she could have a good life. That is why her death was so sorrowful, because when I looked at her in her coffin I saw the tragedy, not because she died, we all die, but because she died in denial of self.

Julia, my *suegra*, caused me no trouble at all except that witnessing her life broke my heart.

When I saw her dead in her coffin, I draped a black lace mantilla around her hair. It was one that she had given me many years before. She gave it to me when I was young and a psuedo-hippie girl, knowing that I would never wear it to mass but would tie it around my head like a gypsy. She gave it to me because I liked it, even though it was the finest mantilla she owned. I was young but not too young to see that she was denying herself a luxury so that I could have it instead.

On the day of her wake, I gave Julia back her black mantilla and entwined my favorite cut crystal rosary around her stiff fingers. It was not enough for me that she was entering heaven with her *guaraches* on. I wanted to her to show up wearing the accoutrements of a *Gran Señora*.

Now, my mother. On the surface she was closer to the suegras that you might see in the telenovela or at the bridal shower in Tijuana. She had the potential of being a bad *suegra*, but she was so astute that she quickly redeemed herself and came around to behaving herself. Like many in her social class, she considered her son a prince and therefore was on the lookout for a princess and when the obligatory princess did not materialize with her name brand clothing and invitations to high society social functions, she was duly disappointed. To my mother's credit, it only took a few months and admonishing looks from my brother before she realized that although my sister-in-law, Celia, was not a society girl, she was a CPA and a damned good one at that. My sister-in-law also loved my brother and my mother was savvy enough to recognize this truth. So, although Celia didn't hold the keys to the Hermosillo Ladies' Social Club, she was a hard working woman, a sensible mother, and loving wife. Celia taught my mother what it meant to be a contemporary and virtuous woman and my mother rose to the occasion.

So on a first-hand basis, I did okay. I had a good *suegra* of my own and my mother, thankfully, did not go to the dark side of *suegra-hood*.

The dark side, I told you was revealed to me in Tijuana, Baja California, when I was seventeen, attending one of those high society bridal showers my mother loved to go to. It was the summer of '69 and I had been sent to be my Tía Ana's companion. Besides driving her to do her shopping and taking her to the hairdresser's, I had nothing to do except read old Spanish novels from my dead uncle's study and sneak into the garden to smoke Eve cigarettes. When the silver-edged baby shower invitation arrived in the mail, Tía Ana bought me a presentable outfit and called me into service as her young attendant.

When we arrived at the Lopez y Lopez household, all the ladies circled round the lead crystal table eating tiny chicken salad sandwiches with the crusts cut off. The bride-to-be was an Anglo girl from Michigan attending San Diego State University, and the groom-to-be was, you guessed it, a prince. Ubaldo, the prince of the family, was also in medical school, a decided double-whammy.

All the ladies were dressed to the nines, which made me grateful that my Tía Ana had bought me the green knit shift and that I wore sheer beige stockings with my patent leather Mary Janes. The bride-to-be was blond; her name was Judith and the ladies buzzed around her like a swarm of bees.

There were gifts neatly stacked in a large white lace parasol on top of a French Provincial table. Ubaldo's mother, aka *La Suegra*, was perfectly coifed and wearing a black and white Chanel Suit.

The Vivaldi in the background accentuated the ambience nicely and the two older gentlemen serving the champagne were dark and wore black uniforms.

After I made sure Tía Ana was comfortable in her Louis XV chair, I sat down next to Judith on the beige brocade sofa.

There was the light clinking of a silver fork on crystal before Judith's *suegra*-to-be started the show. "Now Judith," Señora Lopez y

Lopez announced, "before you open all your gifts, we have three gifts to give you with some special rules, advice you might say, that you must take to make a good marriage."

The other ladies applauded enthusiastically and smiled at each other. My Tía Ana reached over and whispered, "I detest shower games."

La Suegra gave Judith the first gift and Judith gracefully opened it. It was a negligee, gossamer pink with off-white embroidered lace flowers. Judith smiled and the ladies oohed and aahed.

As Judith folded the night gown to put it back in the box and pass it around for the others to see, *La Suegra* said, "Not so fast, dear. There's something else in there."

Judith, unsuspecting soul that she was, reached deeper into the box and pulled out a pair of red crotchless panties with black fur on them. The ladies, all dressed in their day suits with matching shoes, hooted and Judith demurely blushed.

La Suegra looked over to the lady wearing the lime green suit and said, "There are three rules of marriage that we want you to know before you marry my son. My Comadre Gabrielita will tell you the first one."

Comadre Gabrielita took the red crotchless panties from Judith's hand, held them up for all to see and said, "Rule number one — If you want to keep him happy, wear something like this every night and never refuse him sex."

The ladies were whooping it up like the monkeys we had just gone to see at the San Diego Zoo. I looked over to my Tía Ana and she was fanning herself with her black fan. Judith kept a plastic smile on her face but her platinum bangs were wet and I saw her wipe the sweat off her brow.

The second gift was in a small box with a blue bow. Comadre Ernestina, in a flowered chintz suit, stood and watched over Judith as she pulled out a pair of baby blue booties. She went on to tell Judith and the rest of us that although it really was up to God, the best thing you could hope for is to have a boy first. She told us about the time her first son was born and how her husband came to pick her up at the hospital in the new yellow Cadillac that she drives today. There was more approving applause and Judith's face looked pinched.

Doña Tenchita was assigned the presentation of the third gift. "Now, you may be able to wear beautiful lingerie and as far as crotchless panties go, we have signed you up to receive the Frederick's of Hollywood catalog." The howls reached a feverish pitch. I kept looking over to my Tía and noticed that she had glazed over in one of those naps she took with her eyes wide open. Judith was squirming around in her place on the beige brocade couch, and I kept trying to make eye contact with her, but similar to my Tía Ana, she had a faraway look on her face.

"You are a beautiful blonde," Doña Tenchita said, "and I'm sure you can keep Ubaldo interested … for a while, anyway … and of course, we want you to be blessed with a boy first … but just as important as keeping him interested and giving him an heir is what is contained inside this box."

Judith's eyes were beginning to water and I felt really sorry for her so I reached over and put my hand on her knee as Doña Tenchita went on. She picked up a large box from under the coffee table. The box was wrapped in white and silver paper printed with wedding bells.

"So it is all well and good to be blonde and beautiful and take your claim to the Lopez y Lopez name, but if you don't know how to use what's in this box, dear, you might as well go back to Michigan."

The collective response to Doña Tenchita's sneer sounded like the automatic laugh track of a situation comedy.

Judith finally looked at me and I took her hand. It was odd because no one seemed to notice that a: Judith was about to start crying and b:

I was holding her hand like she was going to undergo a painful medical procedure. All that mattered to them was the third rule.

Doña Tenchita placed the heavy box on Judith's lap. I let go of her hand. "Open it." The older woman commanded.

Judith looked around like a tormented deer and I told her, "It's the last gag gift. Just go ahead and get it over with."

Judith carefully removed the large silver bow from the box and slowly peeled the scotch tape from each of the pointed corners of the wrapping paper. She reached in and removed the white tissue paper and pulled out a large red earthenware pot. She looked around and said, "Thank you," to the crowd, and looked at me with a quizzical look.

There was the laugh track again.

"Do you know what this is for my dear?" Tenchita asked.

Judith shook her head , "no."

"Now, that's a problem," Tenchita said to the continued amusement of the chorus.

"You don't have any idea what this is for?"

Judith bit her lip and whispered, "no."

"A ver mijita," Tenchita said including me in the conversation. "What is this? Can you tell Judith?"

"It's a *cazuela*," I said.

"Smart girl," Tenchita said, "And? What's it for?"

"To make food," I said, but I still didn't get the third rule.

"Well, let's get on with it," Tenchita said. "This, Judith," she said, only she pronounced it 'Yudit.' "This is a *cazuela* and it is to be used for one thing and one thing only and that is to refry beans. If you don't know how to make *frijoles*, you might as well finish law school and find a gringo like yourself to marry. No self-respecting wife of a Mexican man does not know how to make a good pot of *frijoles*! So as soon as you come back from your Caribbean cruise, you are going to march back into your *suegra's* kitchen and we are going to hold you hostage like Repunzel in the fairy tale and not let you go until you make the perfect pot of refried beans!"

Judith's eyes were red and she got up to leave.

"Wait a minute!" Tenchita cried out. "Where do you think you're going?"

Judith said, "To the bathroom."

"But we're not done yet. You have to tell us what you thought of the three rules. We are imparting wisdom here, you can't just get up and go to the bathroom."

Judith ran down the hallway.

My Tía Ana gave me a look to go see if she was okay.

I followed Judith to the bathroom but she had already closed the door. I tapped on it lightly and said, "Judith, it's me. Open the door."

Her eyes were running with black mascara as she wiped her face with a wet monogrammed hand towel.

"Are you okay?

"That was awful."

"Shower games are stupid," I said.

"That was really mean," she said and started crying again.

I didn't really know what to say, so I said what any 17-year-old would say in the summer of 1969. "They were fucking with your head."

"Is it because I'm Anglo?"

"That and you're taking Junior," I said.

Judith was blonde, but she wasn't dumb. She looked at me as if she understood and her eyes stopped floating in her head. She washed her face and all her make-up came off and I could see that her skin was ruddy and not like porcelain at all.

"Is it true? she asked.

"True about what?"

"About the beans and that giant pot?"

"No," I said, "you can use a smaller pot."

When we came out of the bathroom, Judith's *suegra*-to-be was waiting in the hallway with open arms. "Come here darling. I'm sorry — Ubaldo didn't tell me you were so sensitive. We didn't mean to make you cry. Here, here," she said, puckering her hot red lips, "let's go open your gifts. I'm sure the rest of them are in much better taste … "

The rest of the gifts were lovely and in much better taste, and the lemon cake was light and delicate. But as I looked around the well-appointed French Provincial room, I knew that Judith, as the gringos say, was not going to have good *suegra* karma.

LA MUJER DE MALA LECHE

· · · · · · · · · ·

THE WOMAN WITH SOUR MILK

MORE IS EXPECTED FROM WOMEN WHEN IT COMES TO LOVING. Just like men have it in their collective memories to hunt, we have it in ours to nurture. Even with all the attempts at redefining gender roles and expectations, much of our value as women is tied up with how well we mother, how sweet our milk is. A *mujer de mala leche* is a woman with sour milk. She may be bitter and cold. She may be crazy. She may be one mean bitch.

My Comadre Liz and I once wrote up a portrait of a *mujer de mala leche* of the worst kind. She was an upper middle class Mexican female, a *popi*, who cared more about appearances, status, and conventions than her children. You wanted to make this woman happy? Buy her an Ethan Allen couch. It didn't matter that the couch was purchased with her son-in-law's drug smuggling money or that her daughter had to get in debt to buy it. It mattered that it was blue and beige brocade and wasn't on sale. Liz and I had fun drawing this picture of a mother who forgot her daughters' birthdays and demanded a monthly "compensation" from each of her adult sons. This "was right and just," she said, after all she'd been through to raise the bunch of them. At first we called her Doña Cashimira because she preferred cashmere over any other kind of wool, but then we settled on Doña Minky for obvious reasons. We howled when we put her in a wheelchair because by the time we got through vilifying her, we were ready to push her down a steep hill.

It is such an aberration, this concept of the woman with sour milk, yet it seems to be a universal occurrence. My friend Miriam says Jews have them, too, these bad mothers. She told me about her Great Aunt Eppie who even had whiskers and intermittently spoke in a man's voice. This woman was so mean she stole her own daughter's jewelry and sold it at a pawn shop.

Mothers are supposed to be benevolent; their milk is supposed to be sweet, but just like there are good ones, there are bad ones, too.

My childhood friend, Pepper, who is half Yaqui and half African-American, told me that her Aunt Pinchi, who helped raise her, was so mean that the children ran from her when she came up the road, like she was the bogeyman. She was the queen of the pinched cheek; she pinched your cheek so hard, it made your eyes water even if you had nothing to cry about.

And listen, I knew a man who married a woman who hated children. She said it outright before he married her and he still brought his two girls to live with them. Straight out of Grimm's, only in the 20th Century. They all lived miserably together for 15 years. Without her help, he bought the prom dresses and the matching shoes, made the chicken soup, and kissed the girls good night. The wife collected porcelain dolls and wouldn't let the girls touch them. When the girls grew up and left home, he finally got fed up and left her for a younger woman.

But it's easy to talk about other people's bad mothers. Other people's mothers can be loosely drawn caricatures that make us laugh, but when it comes to making sense out of our own experience, we cannot take it so lightly.

For years, I tried to figure out Nana Concha, my maternal grandmother. While the rest of the women who inhabited my world kept their dark side in check, hers was out in the open and openly talked about. None of my aunts nor even my mother ever actually said that my grandmother's milk was bad; that would have been a terrible breach of respect, but the family lore was replete with stories illustrating how downright mean she was.

There was the time that she locked my grandfather out of the house the night of his mother's wake. He had to pound on the door to get in and woke up half the neighborhood.

There was the time she stole my mother's monogrammed sheets while my mother fought for her life during the dramatic birth of my older brother. My mother, after spending three weeks in the hospital, went home to find her sheets were missing, and so naturally, she fired the maid. The rediscovery of the missing sheets was made after my mother washed her hands in my grandmother's bathroom and had to reach into the *ropero* to get a towel. She found the sheets, with the monogram part cut out, tucked away behind the towels.

There was the time that my brother Juabeto and I were children and wouldn't take our siesta and my Nana dressed up like La Llorona and came out of the back room where she kept all the saints, scraping her feet against the rough cement floor, moaning and groaning like a monster. I screamed and cowered in the corner and my brother recognized her shoes and whispered to me not to worry. He played along by proceeding to hit her with the broom. When they tried to punish him later, he defended himself by saying that as far as he was concerned he was protecting his baby sister from being eaten alive by La Llorona.

There was the time she bought me the little green plastic box with barrettes of all shapes and colors and then hid them from me in that same *ropero* where my mother discovered her stolen sheets. And there was the time that she told my cousin Pancho that his real father was the old black man who sold vegetables out of a truck.

My father, who was not particularly fond of his mother-in-law, had this to say when my Nana poured petroleum on my little sister's finger when she almost sliced it off on Doña Chana's rusty fence. In response to my mother's tirade about how cruel her mother was, my father said that it wasn't cruelty that drove Nana to such bizarre behavior, but ignorance.

Recalling the offenses that my grandmother allegedly performed and some that I experienced first-hand, I wondered how she got that way. Was it ignorance, as my father said, meanness as my mother said, or according to the likes of Oprah Winfrey, mental illness?

I drove from Santa Fe to Nogales with the specific reason of querying my Tía Chiqui who is married to my grandmother's favorite son and always tells the truth. "So, what do you think, tía?" I asked, "Was she ignorant, mean, or crazy?"

"You could say she was ignorant or mean," she said. "And today, your grandmother would certainly be considered mentally ill. But rather than looking at it that way, I would ask you to understand how she suffered and how that suffering shaped how she treated others.

"Women in the days of your grandmother had it hard. If you were poor and you were a woman, you didn't have many choices. You had to get married and you had to be pure. An impure woman could not live a good life, and if something happened to make a woman impure, even rape, you were ruined. There was the revolution and the terror that girls, like your Nana in those days, lived with every day. You think Pancho Villa was some kind of hero now with all that they've taught you at the university? He was like a beast that scoured the countryside. Your grandmother was forced to shave her head and wear men's clothes just so she could go to the *mercado*. Between the Yaqui raids and the Villistas who would kidnap young women and force them to travel with them as their maids and sex slaves, she had quite a lot to be fearful of. By the time she was 12, she had taken charge of all her younger brothers and sisters. Because she was the eldest daughter, she was more like a servant than a daughter.

"There were many trials that your Nana had to go through but the worst was when her baby brother drowned in the *acequia*. She always blamed herself and it didn't help that both her mother and father blamed her as well."

"How did you know?" I asked, because in all the stories of how mean my Nana was, no one had ever told me about the baby who drowned in the *acequia*.

"She told me." Tía Chiqui said. "When she got older, she would tell me things that she could remember from her younger days. She told me that it had been a hot day in Ures — one of those sweltering Sonoran days when the air was so still it made you dizzy. Her brothers had all gone down to float the toy sail boats down the acequia, wading in and out to cool their feet in the water. She had the baby, Beto, in a basket like baby Moses, and she put the basket down under a cotton-wood tree so she could join the fun. She was sure she put the basket up against the tree and far enough away from the flowing water that the baby would be safe. The baby was sleeping peacefully and when he slept, he slept for a long time.

"She went on to chase the miniature boats made of match boxes with rags for sails, and was having so much fun running barefoot on the cool grass that grew on the banks, that she forgot about the baby. When she got back to the cottonwood tree, the basket was empty. No one knows how the baby got out. The basket might have tipped over. He hadn't even learned to crawl. They found him tangled in a snag of weeds and tree roots downstream.

"They say that your great grandfather was so full of grief that he got on his horse that very day and left his wife and five children to fend for themselves. They say that he was afraid of what he might do to your Nana if he stayed. He might be tempted to beat her to death or throw her in the reservoir to see how well she could swim if left alone to die in the water the way she left her baby brother. The family was all but ruined. Your great grandmother, Altagracia, turned into a ghost, tending to her duties in a stupor, so devastated was she by losing her baby and her husband on the same day.

"Because Gilberto was her *consentido*, her favorite son, and I was his wife, I got to know her well, not like a daughter, but more like a friend. I came to see your Nana as something broken that couldn't be put back together again. We only have these few pieces to help us understand. You are a woman now, Ani, and you can understand and even forgive her for what she did or didn't do."

Something happened when my Tía Chiqui called me a woman. It was as if these words, "You are a woman now," lifted a curtain and I was no longer a frightened child. Prior to this trip to find out more about my grandmother, when I went to Nogales, I went back feeling like the little girl that grew up there, but today, the magic words, "you are a woman," lifted the spell. The spell is this incomplete picture I had of my grandmother. I had this composite of who she was based in part, on what I was told and in part, on what my brother, sister, cousins, and I had experienced. But all of these pieces did not form the whole. What was missing all these years was my ability to look upon what happened not as a child but as an adult.

As my Tía Chiqui handed me more of these broken pieces of the puzzle that was my grandmother, I believed what my wise aunt was telling me, that my grandmother's inexplicable actions and her crazy superstitions were a manifestation of her suffering. Try as she might, she couldn't pass her milk on sweetly.

Looking back to all the other *mujer de mala leche* stories and portraits of bad mothers that I have heard and retold, I came to see that behind the bitterness is a wounded woman. It is the unhealed wound that makes the milk turn sour.

As I left Nogales to come back to Santa Fe, I felt complete with what I found in my adult journey to understand my grandmother and her *locuras*. I came home with the gratitude of understanding Nana Concha more than I ever had before. I also came home with the gratitude of understanding that because I had a whole clan of women caring for me, I could discern the difference between what I could pass on and what I had to leave behind.

LA MALINCHE

• • • • • • • • • •

TRAITOR, AND MOTHER OF MEXICO

LOOK, WHO COULD ARGUE THAT WE MEXICANS HAVE PROBLEMS? I remember once when I lived in Tucson, there was a Jewish baker who burned his bakery down, clearly because he needed the insurance money. It was front page news in the *Tucson Daily Star*, a full-page story, with a picture of the bakery in flames, and another of the diminutive rabbi with a look of kindness mixed with grief. The reporter covering the story interviewed the rabbi.

The rabbi said, "Sam's a good man — he just had problems."

We had a good laugh, my Mexican friends and I. If Sam had been a Mexican, we would've said, "He was a crook and we knew it all along. *Se lo va a llevar la chingada por pendejo.*" (He screwed himself because he's a fool.)

We self-deprecate.

And look what happened when Artu, my first husband, burned his hands with boiling olive oil in Portugal. I called the concierge of the condominium where we were staying and they whisked him off to the local emergency room. The staff placed him first in line because he was a foreign visitor. The moaning lady and the screaming baby had to wait, and it was out of pure politeness and hospitality that they did this. The doctor took good care of him — bandaged his hands and gave him cod liver oil cream and clean bandages to dress his wounds.

The concierge drove us back to the condo and the next day had flowers and a toy for our two-year-old daughter delivered to our door. When I got back to the states, true to the form of a self-deprecating Mexican, I said to my brother, "In Mexico, they would have chopped off his hands."

"No, Sis," he said, "in Mexico they would have arrested him, then chopped off his hands."

You see how we self-deprecate? And it springs from our own self-loathing, born of original sin played out, not by Adam and Eve, but by Cortes and La Malinche.

They blame her for defiling Mexico from its inception because it was her alleged rape that gave birth to the nation. There you have our creation story — Mexico conceived by rape. That's where the expression, *Se chingó la patria*, —"The country is fucked," comes from, and why they call her *La Chingada* — the raped one. It is our original sin and where our shame, *la vergüenza*, comes from. It is the foundation of the self-deprecating thing we Mexicans do. The root meaning of "everything is going south." Octavio Paz wrote a whole book about it and it took me years to figure out what the old guy was saying. I would have simply said that Mexicans suffer from low self-esteem, and he took us into *The Labyrinth of Solitude*.

The dark legacy of La Malinche is blamed for everything from the repulsion of self, to self-shame, to the rampant lack of respect exhibited towards women, to ethnic *envidia*. Ethnic *envidia* is practically a bona fide sociological term now. Some guy by the name of Navarrete from Los Angeles, the second largest Mexican city in the world, wrote an essay on ethnic *envidia* and the *Los Angeles Times* was only too happy to publish it. After that, the concept of ethnic envy took off like a Malcom Gladwell wildfire. Now, everyone knows that Mexicans suffer from a form of a collective self-betrayal.

And this has been attributed to the legacy of La Malinche, the raped mother of Mexico.

I didn't know who Malinche was until I was about 17 years old and witnessed an argument that my mother had with her best friend whom she called sister — *hermana*, and we called *tía*. These two loved each other and would do anything for one another, yet they were always in competition. They were jealous of each other's bodies and one-upped each other on their respective children. They had an ongoing but secret argument conducted through the help of their friends about who had a flatter stomach and better taste in clothes.

When the Mexican government nationalized the petroleum industry, my mother, who loved America, was angry at the expulsion of U.S. corporations from Mexico. My Tía Olga was in favor of keeping the resources in what she mistakenly perceived would be Mexico's coffers. The argument over heated when my mother told her that it wasn't the Mexican people who were going to benefit, but the crooks who engineered the take-over. Take-over meant just that, she said. They were going to take it over and put it in their pockets, buy more girdles for their wives and jewels for their mistresses. My Tía Olga then called my mother, a *malinchista*, a traitor, who would sell Mexico for a few pieces of gold like Judas, "like Malinche did for that one miserable house that Cortes built for her on Higueras Street in Mexico City."

My mother laughed and said, "You're right. I am a *malinchista* and proud of it. As far as I'm concerned, Malinche was a survivor who knew what to do to get herself out of a bad situation. Where is the shame in that? And the Spaniards? They did us a favor when they stopped the carnage. And then came the Gringos who brought us toilets and running water and to them I say 'thank you' and to you I say — 'Después de dios, los gringos,' — the Gringos after God!'"

They didn't speak to each other for at least a week.

My mother's tirade was my official introduction to La Malinche. I was surprised to hear my mother give such an ardent defense of this woman whom I had never heard of. It was after the fight with my Tía Olga that my mother told me about La Malinche. The story we were told, she said, the one about La Malinche being raped and then turning into a traitor, didn't make sense. If La Malinche was taken by force, she said, she sure had a funny way of showing it. She gave me this version of the story.

La Malinche was a Nahua Indian girl who was sold into slavery to another tribe by her mother so her brother, upon their father's death, could take over the village. When Cortes arrived (and make no mistake, he was drop-dead gorgeous), the Aztecs, poor suckers (*pobres cabrones*), thought he was a god by the name of Quetzalcoatl. Believing that Cortes was a savior god, they showered him with gifts of gold and about a dozen slave girls. Malinche was among them. But Cortes was no Quetzlcoatl; he was the *mero mero chingón* sent by the Spanish Empire. He brought with him soldiers and priests to conquer land for Spain and souls for the church but somewhere along the line they ended up with rape and pillage, which by my mother's account, was not unusual in those days when the Europeans were conquering the world. When Cortes first laid eyes on La Malinche, my mother said, it was love at first sight. She was as beautiful as he was handsome and she spoke two languages, Nahuatl and Maya.

Cortes, not being stupid, *ningún pendejo*, seized the day, and Mexico and all its treasures along with it. One of Cortes's countrymen, a priest who had been enslaved by the Indians and subsequently freed, spoke Maya and Spanish. So between Malinche's knowledge of Nahuatl and Maya, and Father Geronimo's knowledge of Maya and Spanish, Cortes was able, with the additional help of diseases like smallpox and syphilis, to conquer Mexico: the land for Spain and its souls for the Catholic church.

La Malinche was referred to as *La Chingada* — the raped one, but the rape part, according to my mother, did not add up. La Malinche had been betrayed by her family — sold to slavery by her own mother and then given away like an object to Cortes. Did he rape her? "Think about this," my mother said. "Was having sex with a woman against her will considered wrong by anyone's standards anywhere in the world in 1521? If you believe that, *hija*, you know *mierda* about history."

Even with my mother unpacking the Malinche myth, the issue still remains. Do we as Mexicans accept *malinchismo* as a national characteristic?

I didn't come to know the intellectual explanation of La Malinche until I read *The Labyrinth of Solitude* in college and read Octavio Paz's account of Malinche and Cortes and the destiny that their union brought to Mexico. Paz explains this succinctly by reminding us that if you want to insult a Spaniard, you call him, *"Hijo de puta,"* son of a whore. But if you want to insult a Mexican, you call him *"Hijo de la chingada,"* son of a raped woman. Somewhere in our tragic Mexican amalgamation, we believed those who said that we needed to be ashamed of ourselves because we were *los hijos de la chingada*, the sons and daughters of rape and domination.

But what if it was a lie? What if La Malinche was not raped? What if she, *ninguna pendeja*, with her command of languages and with the help of Father Geronimo, willingly acted as Cortes' interpreter and did what she thought was the right thing to do to survive? What if all she did was figure it out?

LA PUTA

· · · · · · · · · ·

THE WHORE

I NEVER KNEW MUCH ABOUT PUTAS except that being a *puta* is about the worst thing you could be and having people believe you're a *puta* was almost as bad. It wasn't so much that I could become one as much as people would think I was one. They would get what my mother called the wrong idea. That's one of the reasons I had to take a chaperone everywhere I went. The chaperone was supposed to protect me and my reputation from going down the wrong road. The way I understood it, there were several wrong roads a girl could take. There was the wrong road of a boy taking advantage of you, having sex with you when you didn't know any better. If that happened, one consequence was getting pregnant. If you got pregnant in those days, you had to get married if you were a decent girl. If you didn't get married, you brought shame to your family, not to mention a baby for them to raise. There were very few unwed mothers and giving birth to a bastard marred you in the eyes of everyone, starting with those ladies who looked like wasps in the social pages of the newspaper. If you were one of those unlucky ones that got pregnant but didn't get the boy to marry you, even if you weren't a *puta*, many people would believe you were. So in effect, you and your family were defiled.

Then there was the wrong road of you having sex and wanting more and possibly even with various boys, which meant you were well on your way of being a genuine *puta*. (You notice how freely I use the word *puta*? That's because I have been liberated, thanks to *Gringolandia*, but we were not allowed to use the word *puta*. (We could spell it, P-U-T-A, but we couldn't say it.) I didn't quite understand all the different wrong roads that branched out of being a genuine *puta*, only some. One was— *el callejón de los chingasos* — *Chingaso* Alley. That meant that if you became a *puta*, you would be abused, ridiculed, beaten up, and/or generally mistreated. The other alley was becoming a professional *puta*, a prostitute, and being exiled to Canal Street for the rest of your life like a prisoner.

Canal Street was a designated district where prostitutes were allowed to live and work. The government controlled their lives — they were only allowed to leave Canal Street and go into town once a week, usually on Tuesdays, when they got their blood test at the health department and went to the movies. They lived their entire lives in *la zona roja* — the red (*puta*) zone.

On a couple of Tuesdays, Gilda Hodgers and I went to the Cine Royal, not to watch the movies as much as to watch the *putas*. We wanted to see what they were really like. We felt naughty like when we looked up the word, "fornication" in the dictionary, but we were ultimately disappointed because for the most part, they looked like everyone else except with more make-up.

All this information came down to one thing. A girl like me needed protection. It started with the chaperone and got more sophisticated from there. I had what you could call round-the-clock-surveillance. On the front line was my little sister, better known as "*La Plaga* — The Plague.* She was 10 and took her job seriously and knew I wasn't supposed to kiss or even hold hands. She would hide under the dining room table to spy when Art came *de visita* to make sure I didn't go down the wrong road. But there was no real chance of that because they had other safeguards in place. For one thing, I had already been indoctrinated through instructional stories to the world of good girls and bad girls — virgins and whores.

There was the story about the bad girl who had a horn on her forehead and the good girl who had a star. The bad girl, like Pinocchio, was cursed with a horn that grew when she was bad, no matter what she did to disguise it. When she did bad things, the horn grew. I, you guessed it, had a star on my forehead and an entire clan of people to see to it that it remained there.

To reinforce the story of the girl with the star versus the girl with the horn, my mother repeatedly told me the story about the boy who fell in the gutter and wiped the slime and mud off, got up, and went on his way. The girl who fell in the gutter couldn't clean herself off for anything. The moral of the tale was that people will give boys second chances, but not girls. The girl who falls in the gutter can't clean herself off no matter what. Like bad carpet, you clean the stain and the stain just keeps resurfacing. If you take the wrong road and became a *puta*, there are no second chances.

Finally, my mother told me that I was her little pearl and she was the shell. It was her job to see to it that the shell wasn't opened before its time. She wanted the pearl to float out of the shell when it was ready; she didn't want anyone prying it open and ruining it forever.

Besides the protection of chaperones and cautionary tales, my big brother could track me down in his 1962 Mustang. Then there were my uncles, who in their daily comings and goings kept their eye out for me. For example, if they saw me walking down the street alone, they would stop and pick me up and take me to where I needed to go with an emphatic, "Why didn't you call me? I would have taken you." Then they would see me safely home.

I never knew much about *putas* except that all the forces of my universe were poised to protect me from being one or being perceived as one. The rest of what I learned about *putas*, I learned in Tucson from Evelyn Lopes when I was fresh out of college and had gotten a job as a Vocational Rehabilitation Counselor.

It was 1977 and Evelyn Lopes, pronounced like "ropes" she said, was one of my first clients. Evelyn had heard that Voc Rehab could help her change professions and so she called to make an appointment.

I explained that Vocational Rehabilitation was a service provided to people who had a disability that constituted a handicap to employment. Why did she think she was eligible for Vocational Rehabilitation?

She said that she was a hooker with a back problem and couldn't screw like she could when she was younger and more able-bodied.

With the straight face that they told me to use with junkies and con artists, I told her that prostitution was not considered a legitimate profession, not in the Dictionary of Occupational Titles sort of way, and that I didn't think I could justify providing services to someone who had an illegal profession. I told her I was sorry but I couldn't help her.

She said, "Can't you tell them I'm an exotic dancer and can't shake my booty anymore because of my sciatica?"

"Are you a dancer?" I asked.

She rolled her eyes and said, "Sure, why not."

I wasn't quite sure how to build Evelyn's case, so I went to one of my colleagues who had been conducting shady casework for years, and he told me what to do. I sent Evelyn to an aging orthopedic surgeon around the corner on Congress Street, who, my colleague assured me, would give me the diagnosis I needed. Dr. Luna, apparently one of Evelyn's most devoted clients, wrote in his summary that Evelyn was an exotic dancer with a herniated disc who couldn't do what was required of her anymore in her present profession, therefore, he recommended retraining. My supervisor signed off on it and I opened the case.

I wrote Evelyn a letter and told her that we had determined that she was eligible for services and to come in to do an Individualized Rehabilitation Plan.

The first time she came in for the IRP, she sat down and asked me, "So, am I your first *puta*?"

With the same poker face that I had used before, I said no, that I had been raised in Nogales where we had a red light district.

"Bastards," she said, and lit a cigarette.

I told her that she couldn't smoke in my office because I was sensitive to cigarette smoke and she said, "How delicate of you," and stomped the cigarette out on the floor. I pretended not to notice.

She wanted to be a barber, she said, and could I send her to barber school? I told her no, that being a barber meant she had to stand all day, and how could we justify that vocational goal if she had a bad back?

I recommended that she go to a short-term training program at this place called V-TEP where she could get trained as a receptionist and eventually do her job sitting down.

She said, " I can dig it." In addition to being 50 years old, Evelyn was hip, if a bit passé for 1977; she wore Indian prints and love beads and said things like "far out" and "groovy." From her appearance, you would have thought she was African-American, but she said that her mother was Mexican and she didn't know who her father was except that he was Portuguese, thus the Lopes pronounced like "ropes." She smelled of patchouli oil and had a nose ring from when she saved up her money one year and went to India.

Although according to the terms of the Individualized Rehabilitation Plan, I didn't have to hear from Evelyn but once a month for a progress report, she stopped in to see me every Monday morning at 8:30 before her training program started. She would tell my secretary that she was here for her counseling session and would come in with two cups of chai. I knew as much about chai as I did about *putas* or counseling. I had never had chai before I met Evelyn and had taken exactly one counseling course in college and never attended.

I didn't ask Evelyn why she wanted counseling or what she thought I could do for her. Our sessions were more like half-hour chats and they didn't seem that difficult. I figured Evelyn needed something from me, and although I didn't know what or how to provide it, I would try my best. She joked around with me and called me Polly Ana.

One day she came in and said, "Look, if you and I are going to understand each other, you are going to have to improve your *putología*. It's a little flawed." She told me that she had been an honest *puta*, unlike other women she knew who pretend they weren't.

She read my confused face, and without waiting for a verbal response she said, "Okay, Polly Ana, do you know women who have sex with their husbands, not because they love them, but because their husbands pay for everything?"

I shrugged and said, "I suppose."

"*Putas,*" she said. "It's an exchange of money for services, money for sex, prostitution. They don't even like their husbands anymore but they spread 'em anyway."

She told me that she had a young friend, just 28, who married a geezer about 72 years old and the only reason she married him was that she was poor and the guy had money. "There are a lot of whores out there," she said. "I'm just one of the honest ones."

That afternoon after work, my friend Carmen and I went to the shopping mall and ran into Shelly, a woman we had gone to high school with. Shelly was with her new husband. Carmen reported that Shelly's husband was a successful lawyer from Culiacán, Sinaloa. Shelly looked like Mr. T — with so many gold chains around her neck.

Carmen made me laugh when she told me they called the lawyer *"El posole,"* because he had so much acne on his face, he looked like a bowl of hominy stew. We were polite and said hello to the woman but all I could hear inside my head was Evelyn whispering *"puta, puta, puta."*

After running into Mr. and Mrs. Posole, I came to a conclusion about Evelyn. She was intelligent and analytical, and I liked her. Against everyone's advice and my own better judgment, I decided that Evelyn and I could be friends.

The next time she came in I told her about my epiphany about Mrs. Posole. I told her it was thanks to her tutorial on *putología* that I could see it now. She smiled and sat down. I went on attempting to share the insight that was sparked by her explanation, when I noticed she crossed her arms in front of her chest.

"So I realized you're right. There are a lot of whores and not all of them are women," I went on. "It is a unisex phenomenon … I mean, men do it too, right?"

"Suit yourself, Polly," she said.

Evelyn had something on her mind and she only had 20 minutes to get to it so I shut up.

She had been professional, she said, and she didn't give it away, she sold it. Then she asked, "Aren't you going to take notes?"

I grabbed a yellow pad.

No one took anything from her that she didn't want to give; she was in charge. She did it because she wanted to and she got money for it and so what? She had never been ashamed of it.

I stared at her and looked at the paper and wrote down a few notes. She got up, mumbled something about being late and left.

Every week Evelyn would come in and do the same thing — give me the cup of chai, sit down, and then divulge something of herself. I began to notice that every time I wanted to talk, she acted disinterested and looked away.

Evelyn was honest with me the way I didn't think anyone could be honest when she told me that at first she "played" with men, then saw that she was pretty good at the game and finally decided to do it professionally. She could keep her own hours and it beat working in the underwear factory.

One of the few times she asked me anything about myself, she said, "You're a good girl, aren't you? You play everything by the book."

"Not everything," I said.

"Like what?" she asked. "What's the worst thing you've ever done?"

I told her that the worst thing I had ever done was watch one of my classmates put LSD into one of our teacher's drinks in high school.

"Okay, that's pretty bad," she said.

"I know. The teacher hallucinated and thought he was going crazy. I still feel terrible about it," I said, "but then he was this old guy that would drop his eraser and look up our skirts. He did this dozens of time during our class period. All the girls had to cover their legs with their sweaters. My mother went in to complain and they ignored it. The administration knew he was a pervert and didn't do anything about it."

"Pricks," is all she said.

Evelyn kept coming to see me every week and I found myself looking forward to it. It was the most interesting thing that happened to me on Monday mornings. It annoyed me, however, that Evelyn was more interested in speaking than in listening. I had to remind myself that she was, after all, my client and not my friend.

It was about the eighth week of our counseling sessions when she came in and sat silent for a few moments. By then I had figured out that perhaps the warnings that I had heard about counselors being friends with their clients were true, so I was trying to be more professional.

"It started when I was six years old and my grandfather would come into this old camper that he had turned into a playhouse," she said finally.

I waited.

I thought I had missed something … "I'm sorry?"

"He touched me," she said. "You don't have to ask where, do you?"

"No," I said.

"I wanted to tell my mom, but he told me she would beat me for being such a *birrionda*."

"*Birrionda?*" I asked.

"What? You don't know that word?" She asked.

I stared at her. I didn't know how to answer, so I sat there, remembering that I had heard my grandmother use this word to refer to one of those girls that had gone down the wrong road on Calle Rosario. It meant a girl who teases men. I wondered how a little girl of six could be a tease and my impulse was to get up from behind my desk and hold her, but she sat there like a stone, speaking these words to me, and I felt equally paralyzed.

"He told me he would burn the playhouse," Evelyn said. With her eyes cast down she went on to tell me that she hated his rough and scratchy hands, and the way he smelled made her throw up once.

"How long did this go on?" I asked, feeling inadequate.

"He died when I was eight," she said, "of a massive heart attack." She was secretly glad he died, she said, but never told anyone what happened. "You can write that down, if you like," she said, looking at the old pocket watch she wore around her neck. "I have to go," she said, and dashed off.

I was still stunned, when a week later she came in and told me that when she was 16 she had been doing "it" with lots of boys in school in secret and her youngest uncle found out. I thought she was going to tell me that her uncle was upset and demanded to know what she was doing and why, but she said that it was then that her uncle came after her. "After me," is what she said and I didn't quite understand what she meant by "after me" until she told me that something weird happened when her uncle came after her. She liked it and didn't want it to stop.

The week before when Evelyn first told me about her grandfather, I went to the textbook that I kept from the counseling class I didn't attend. I read about a technique called "reflective listening." It seemed appropriate for me to use it this time, while Evelyn was telling me about her uncle.

I said, "So it started with your grandfather, and then when you were 16, your uncle also sexually abused you … "

Evelyn's green eyes turned a bright yellow when she yelled out, "Oh stop!" and got up from her chair. "You missed a few beats, Polly," she said. "My uncle was not sexually abusing me. I knew exactly what I was doing!"

I should've backed off, but I was appalled. "But you were just a child, a 16-year- old girl!"

She had a look of disgust as she went to the door. She turned around and hissed at me. "Look, stupid. You may have been a child when you were 16, but I wasn't. I did whatever the fuck I wanted when I was 16! And if I wanted to fuck my uncle, it's none of your business!"

"I'm sorry," I said. "I only meant … "

"I know what you meant." she said, and left.

That was the end of Monday mornings with Evelyn. I would get positive reports from V-TEP that she was doing well and that they were sure they could place her in a job consistent with her vocational goal.

Three months later, I got the final report stating that Evelyn had been placed as a receptionist at an upscale Chinese restaurant on Speed-way Boulevard — the House of the Seven Dragons.

I decided that it was appropriate to go pay her a visit, congratulate her on her accomplishments and apologize for my lack of training and experience. I bought her a potted purple orchid and a card. I wrote a note in the card saying that I had mishandled the case and I wanted to make sure she knew that what happened between us wasn't her fault, but mine.

She was dressed in an ankle-length bright green Chinese satin dress, slit on the side. It accented her dark brown skin and curly black hair. She was sitting on a red lacquer stool talking to an old Chinese gentleman in a gray suit. He didn't appear to speak English, but it didn't seem to matter.

When she saw me come in, she acknowledged me and took the man's arm and escorted him to a corner table.

"I heard congratulations are in order," I said when she came towards me. I handed her the orchid.

"Thank you, Ana," she said, no longer calling me Polly.

"Do you like it here?" I asked, trying to make small talk.

She laughed and said, "It doesn't pay that well, but I have quite a following."

I looked at her quizzically and then immediately regretted it.

She squeezed my shoulder and whispered, "It's okay, really. I'm like a geriatric geisha." She giggled at her own description and then said, "Some of them can't even get it up anymore. It's nice, you know, and it's not so hard on my back."

A tall, dark middle-aged man walked in and waited at the door. I saw Evelyn glance at him.

"I'll go," I said, "you're busy. I just wanted to check in to see how you were doing."

"The work is okay … Sometimes all they want is someone to listen," she said.

"Good luck, Evelyn," I said, reaching out to shake her hand.

I walked away and she followed me to the door. "Ana," she said, "you really did help me, you know."

"I hope so, Evelyn … I wrote a little something on the card. I wanted you to understand that —"

She interrupted. "Listen, I just needed to tell someone. They say it's important to tell at least one person and I picked you."

I looked at her standing there regal and strong and I had the same urge that I had had months ago when she first told me about her grandfather. I wanted to hold her, to offer her comfort, but this time I knew that I needed it more than she.

Before she could see that I was about to cry, I said "Thank you," and walked out into the blinding Tucson sun.

Evelyn Lopes, pronounced like "ropes," was honest with me the way I didn't think anyone could be honest. Everything I didn't know about chai, about *putas*, about counseling, and about listening, I learned from her.

LA NOVIA

· · · · · · · · ·

THE BRIDE

ON THE FIRST ANNIVERSARY OF HER PARENTS DIVORCE, my daughter
and I embarked on our first annual pilgrimage to Spain. No ordinary
pilgrims on our walk to Santiago de Compostela were we. We were
going shopping. On that first trip, while we were both licking our
divorce wounds, one of our greatest and most healing pleasures was to
window-shop for wedding dresses. We shared this pleasure, both of us,
somewhat guiltily. I mean, who are we? Joan and Melissa Rivers? No,
we are two intelligent women. The mother is a feminist, dyed in the
wool by North American feminist theory and burnt to a crisp by the
disillusion of marriage. The daughter, a more ethereal creature, part
Pija, (Spanish American Princess) part wants-to-grow-dreads-but can't
quite give up the clean-hair look, hasn't signed up for being a feminist
quite yet, but there is still hope. Although my daughter hasn't read
Betty Friedan, it is clear to me, after editing a research paper she wrote
on *Sex and the City*, that this woman-child of mine understands sexual
politics. So, why wedding dresses? Why does that Spanish wedding
shop pull us in like a magic door? After spending considerable time
pondering, I realize that the reason it pulls us in like a magic door is
that it is a magic door. I silently ask my daughter, "What if, although it
wasn't true for me, you went through that white passage and found true
and everlasting love?" That is the promise. And although it turned out
to be a myth for the mother, the daughter should decide for herself.

That year in Barcelona, we saw a wedding gown in a window that had those promises sewn carefully row by row in the softest of white frothy ruffles made of tulle. Let me stop now because "ruffles" does not begin to tell you what this gown was like. Not only was this gown for once a princess, soon to be a queen, no, this heavenly confection would be fitting of the intelligent, successful, loving and well-loved creature who is my daughter. It oozed happiness, faithfulness, and love everlasting, not to mention prosperity and world travel. This was the dress! I remember stopping outside the shop on Passeig de Gracia and hearing angelic trumpets calling and I was not alone.

"Oh my God," Sara said as she swooned.

"I'm going in!" I said, opening the gilded door. The shop smelled like bliss. I asked the beautiful woman with a yellow tape measure around her neck, "How much is the gown in the window?" And she breathily answered that it could be made to fit for 1000 Euros. (Oh, but the dollar was strong then!)

Sara, caught in the spell said, "Let's buy it now. I can find someone to marry later!"

I agreed and said, "The marriage will take care of itself. It's the wedding dress that's important."

Our laughter broke the spell and we thanked the beautiful lady and walked out the door.

"That was close," my daughter said.

"It's the best one so far," I said.

"Let's remember this one," she said.

"Forever," I said, and took her arm to cross the street.

The wedding dress incident on Passeig de Gracia made me think of my own history as a bride.

I resisted being a bride because, at the time, I considered myself a smart cookie with eyes wide open. I was not blind, I insisted. Yes, of course I loved him, but I was practical. And even in my most romantic moments, I just wanted to join Art on a journey. I didn't wear white. The dress was beige and it had embroidered lilac flowers and Las Hermanas Ley made it — two diminutive ladies from the Philippines who lived on top of a cobblestone hill in Nogales, Sonora, supplying the feminine population with proper attire for any occasion.

The Sisters Ley had made my Juliette dress in pink chiffon for my first prom and the dress was a dream. I called it my virgin dress because it was a dress and I was a virgin. They had also made my Heart Fund Ball debutante dress. White Victorian to the max, it hid an emerging hippie girl. But by the time I married, it was only three years after the Virgen Juliette and two years after the Debutante, I wanted to be mother nature or a peacenik and exchange non-traditional vows in my bare feet by Blue Haven Creek. In my spare time I wanted to protest against the war and boycott grapes and yell out "¡Viva La Raza!"

But these are the real reasons my wedding dress was beige and not white: I was not blind to the mother-fucking patriarchy, and I was not a virgin. Not to mention that in those days, wearing white in a Catholic church at a wedding was serious business, and you were a hypocrite if you walked down the aisle in white and offered your flowers to La Virgen when everyone knew that the flowers had already been offered up in the back seat of a car, in my case a 1968 Ford Galaxy. So I wore beige, and Art and I walked together down the aisle.

"No one," I protested "is going to be giving me away, no sir." I was not some commodity. There would be no "Who gives this woman to this man?" monkey business at my wedding. And there would be no veil either, damn it. After all, I was no innocent; I was 20 years old!

So I forfeited bride-hood and went straight to the reality of marriage.

Not long ago, a distant friend of mine was married at 60. She wore a white bridal gown with a veil covering her time-worn face. It was most immediately sad because it felt like she was attempting to reclaim something lost, but in the next breath I cheered up because I, too, believe in the act of reclamation.

If I got married again, which I wouldn't, I would wear a purple dress and it would have a whole lot of stuff going on. I would be the aging purple bride. My dress, among other things, would say, "Today I am in love with a man and he is not perfect. His nose is crooked but his love feels intact even though it is marred by the injuries and curses of the past." And people might applaud the way they do nowadays at weddings, which I think is stupid, but the applause would not be because our message was so hopeful but because it was so true.

I was a reluctant bride at 20. The decision to marry was a functional one. We were starving and we believed Three Dog Night when they told us one was the loneliest number. Art proposed while we were comparison shopping two cans of corn, and we loved each other like two birds love each other in a storm. We had some kind of illusion but it was not white or blind. It was beige, embroidered with the lilac flowers of wishful thinking.

LA HIJA

· · · · · · · · · ·

THE DAUGHTER

I NEVER WANTED A BABY. Growing up on the border of Mexico and the United States in the '60's turned me into a cynical human being. As I grew up to understand the meaning of misery, the contrasts were too sharp and cruel. The chain link fence separated the starving children shining shoes for their next meal from those of us who wore black and white saddle oxfords and went to American schools in post war "Leave it to Beaver" neighborhoods.

The consequences of poverty and overpopulation were in my face every day. It didn't seem fair that I had shoes to wear while the children in my grandmother's neighborhood grew layer upon layer of skin on the bottoms of their feet to run up and down the hills. No, I would never have children.

I finalized my decision when as a girl of 15 I witnessed a baby being given away in the San Juan de Dios market in Guadalajara. He was swathed in a blue crocheted blanket. His mother stood by the fruit stand, offering until someone took him out of her outstretched arms.

Not too much time later, my mother, at the end of her rope because the Red Cross couldn't locate my brother in Viet Nam, went blind. She regained her sight later when they found him alive. The doctor called it hysterical blindness.

Mothers suffer.

Life was too harsh to bring a child into the world. I operated on this premise into adulthood. Me, have a baby? No, gracias. By 30 I had turned myself into a zero population growth advocate. When women talked about the miracle of birth, I thought it was bullshit. I thought they were giving themselves way too much credit. "Any mammal can give birth. What's the big deal?" I said.

But all that changed one hot May afternoon. It was a blistering Arizona day and I had stayed home from work and school. I wasn't so much sick as burnt out. I was tired of working and going to graduate school, tired of commuting from Tubac to Tucson every day in the ever-vibrating chamber of a '71 Volkswagen Karmann Ghia, and tired of the record-breaking heat.

There is an eerie stillness to noon on a hot Arizona desert day. It is quiet to the point of distraction. The heat is a screechy hot. That day, the only sound that I could hear was the buzzing of the cicadas, like a crescendo announcing the day's infernal peak. The noise was so loud that I felt it swelling in my brain. I toyed with the idea of shutting the doors and windows, but that would mean no crosswind. It was miserable and it was only May.

I went into the kitchen to have a glass of iced tea and the cicadas came to an abrupt stop. Silence set in. It was a stillness so spooky, I felt afraid. I tried to shake off the fear by telling myself that I had drunk too much coffee, and what was I doing having more caffeine? I called myself silly and made a mental note to cut down on coffee and meditate.

I went to the front window to look out at the fig tree in my neighbor's yard, a tiny oasis in the vast yard of dry desert gravel. Just as I was thinking that perhaps I should go lie down, I heard the voice of a small child cry out, "Mama!" There were no children on the edge of the village where we lived.

I heard the cry again. "Mama!" And I felt a surge of blood rush to my forehead. Gooseflesh took over my entire body. I felt dizzy and sat down. The cry came from the back of the house so I walked back to the bedroom but the only thing in the back of the house were acres and acres of creosote bush.

I blamed the cry on the ravens, who could imitate anything. I stood at the sliding glass door staring at the field of creosote when I heard it again. "Mama!" This time, it was a playful sing-song cry. It was not a cry of despair, but a cry of joy. It was a baby calling out for her mother. Tears flowed down my cheeks as I stood there — knowing.

It occurred to me just then that I was having one of those wretched *ñañaras*, Mexican shorthand for a message from the beyond. While in my childhood I was devoted to the Blessed Mother, as I grew into a cynical adolescence, she receded into the background and was only consulted in case of emergencies. The kooky tales from my family of women were too much for my emerging modern brain. There were too many claims of psychic powers and presentiments designed to enlighten me and make me wear a bra. I wanted no part of it. I didn't want to be psychic; I wanted to be American.

I sat in the stillness of the hot afternoon, thoroughly creeped-out and anticipating hearing the cry again, but the afternoon was silent again. So silent that I turned on the television to break it.

That afternoon, I waited for Art like I had never waited for him before or since. When he walked in, he must have sensed there was something amiss, because the first thing he said, even before hello, was, "What's wrong?"

I didn't know what I would answer until the moment the words came out of my lips. "I want to have a baby."

"Ha!" he said. "Tell me another one."

I stared at him.

"Are you kidding me?" He knew I wasn't.

"No," I said, " I want to have a baby."

"So when did you come to this decision?"

"Today."

"You're stressed."

"I want to have a baby."

"Haven't we been talking about this for 11 years, how the world is too fucked-up to bring a baby into it? How enough people are having babies and we don't need to add more people to the world?"

"I want to have a baby," I said.

"But what about zero population? What about how irresponsible it is for those of us who know better to bring more children into the world? What about that, huh?"

I told him about the small child crying out in the middle of the day, calling out for her mama.

"Okay, you're nuts. Estás loca."

I started crying again and it poured out like a flood.

"Chingada madre," he said as he took me in his arms.

I knew then that this feeling was more powerful than both our rational minds could handle. I knew it as sure as I have ever known anything.

In an act of surrender he said, "You can't get pregnant until you stop smoking."

"Okay," I said, and started crying again.

We held on to each other and this time we both cried.

That was the last day I ever smoked a cigarette. The following day was Friday and we drove to Rocky Point on the Sea of Cortez. Without my diaphragm. We played like children in the sand. We chased the waves and sang to them and we saw a pair of Osprey in their nest. That was May 23, 1982. Sara was born exactly nine months later.

The worst part about being pregnant was wearing pantyhose. Pantyhose and getting up at six in the morning to teach 8:ooAM freshmen composition to Saudi Arabian students at the University of Arizona. The best part of that was that it was a class of male Saudi Arabian students and once they realized I was pregnant they rolled out the red carpet and never let me lift a finger. If I dropped the eraser, six of them would dive to pick it up. If I said I needed to get a glass of water, they would fight over which one got to fill my cup. Once I even found a yellow daisy on my desk.

While the pregnancy was easy, the labor was hard. Months of Lamaze and self hypnosis, plans for a LaBoyer bath and soft music to give birth to, got me 23 hours of labor and a trip from the Tucson Birth Center to the Tucson Medical Center to have a C-section. The result was a beautiful little mammal with a cone head covered with the darkest, longest hair you've ever seen on a baby.

And when she cried out "Mama!" I knew who she was.

NUESTRA SEÑORA DE GUADALUPE

· · · · · · · · · ·

OUR LADY OF GUADALUPE

FROM THE TOP OF ROSARIO HILL where my Nana lived in Nogales, Sonora, I could see trails of little girls dressed in pastel colored dresses taking flowers down to the Santuario to offer them to The Blessed Mother, Our Lady of Guadalupe. My dress was sky blue and had been made by my beloved Tía Paqui. The sad fact that she was a *quedada* translated to good news for me because she was like my own personal Fairy Godmother. She was soft and big and good and she loved me with all her heart. I knew that if she could make my wishes come true, she would.

Besides being a *quedada*, a kindergarten teacher, a good cook, and my own personal Fairy Godmother, my Paqui was a *Guadalupana*, a member of a society of women who devote themselves to Our Lady of Guadalupe. She was the one who first told me the story of Juan Diego and the series of indignities he had to suffer in order to convince the bishop of Mexico City that Our Lady of Guadalupe had indeed appeared to him on Tepeyac Hill. My Paqui told me about the Basilica, the big church in Mexico City that had been built on the actual site where The Blessed Mother first appeared. She said that to those who believed in the miracle, the Basilica smelled like roses of Castille, the roses that Our Lady materialized so that others would believe in her and the Indians would find refuge from their suffering.

I was lucky about offering flowers because my Nana had a garden. My grandmother's garden consisted of roses, dahlias and various kinds of lesser flowers like daisies, asters, and white yarrow. Although the roses were prized, the dahlias, being less abundant, were the queens of the garden. And when Nana and Paqui cut a bouquet for me to take to The Blessed Mother, they were especially careful with the dahlias. I got only one dahlia per bouquet, usually a big purple one. They wrapped the bouquet in newspaper and warned me not to hold it too close as it would stain my fancy dress with ink.

My Paqui would sometimes go with me and wait in the back of the church while I flung my flowers at the altar like my brother had shown me. He said the flowers would reach farther if I learned how to throw them right. After a few introductory trips to the church to offer flowers, my Paqui let me join the girls that trailed down the hill in procession. I looked back every so often to see her waving from the top of the hill.

I preferred offering flowers to The Blessed Mother to sitting in a hot church full of people at noon on Sundays. Singing *O Maria, madre mía* to the virgin was so much better than trying to figure out what the droning crowd would do during mass. Sit, stand, or kneel? I could never figure it out. The way I saw it, it was better to wear the pretty blue dress and fling my flowers at the altar than to be bored and hot in Sunday mass. I would get so sleepy during Sunday mass that my mom had to tap me with her giant fan so I could wake up. I concluded that Sunday mass was for the Holy Father and offering flowers was for the Blessed Mother.

Offering flowers was fun, and who could deny that the atmosphere on Sundays was austere? The most exciting, albeit embarrassing, thing that happened on Sunday was when Padre Nacho would publicly point to a young woman dressed too scantily and kick her out of the church, admonishing that next time she came to God's house, she should pay more respect and not dress like a woman of ill-repute.

To occupy myself during Sunday mass, I tried to picture God like the nuns had told us to. I saw two images: Jesus bleeding on the cross and an old man with a long white beard sitting on a throne with a white pigeon hovering over his head. Compare that with a sunny day in May, when I dressed up in my sky blue gown, took my bouquet of flowers and marched down to the church singing praises to the Blessed Mother. Compare that to the first time I walked into the Santuario and smelled the roses. In that instant I believed in the miracle, in the apparition of Our Lady of Guadalupe on Tepeyac Hill. Sometimes at the end of the offering, they took us all outside and gave us hot chocolate with cinnamon and the old man with the dancing monkey played his violin while the monkey danced. Who could deny that this was better than going to Sunday mass?

But besides the dress, the flowers, the songs, the chocolate, and the monkey, the Blessed Mother was good and kind and I knew she loved me. Like my Tía Paqui, she was the one who always smiled and said I looked fine, I was smart, no I wasn't fat, I was just right.

At night, when I prayed to the Blessed Mother to keep me safe from the bad dog that tried to bite me in the morning when I went to buy bread, I felt a whisper on my cheek. "There, there," she said, until I fell asleep.

When my tía Gloria decided to give herself to the Father, the Son, and the Holy Ghost, I wondered why she didn't pick the Blessed Mother instead. She could sing her songs and tell us stories about the Blessed Mother's many appearances. As far as I was concerned, of all the heavenly beings besides an occasional guardian angel, the Blessed Mother was the only one who had bothered to come back to earth. I had not heard of one instance where Jesus appeared out of nowhere in modern times. By contrast, the Blessed Mother had appeared all over the world, even Yugoslavia.

But no, not Jesus. It was almost as if after the resurrection, which happened right after he was crucified, that was it. He ascended into heaven and sat at the right hand of the Father, never to be seen again. It was the Blessed Mother who traveled and told us to pray the rosary and be nice.

That's how it happened. It was that very afternoon when I walked in to the church in my sky blue dress and smelled the roses. That's when the Blessed Mother came inside me and she's lived here ever since. I never had to invite her into my heart like they tell you to do on TV with Jesus. The Blessed Mother got into my heart and I think of her every time I smell roses, or taste Mexican chocolate or hear those old hymns I sang with all those little girls dressed in party dresses.

I can see her sometimes as she watches over me; she is on the left side of the horizon. She has become so much a part of my landscape that when I find the world is closing in, I see her smile, and I feel her whisper on my cheek. "There, there," she says, and I know I can handle whatever comes my way.

She comes to me now in various ways, subtle and obvious. I build shrines here and there. She is in the garden tied to the bush by a piece of jute to keep the wind from toppling her over. There she is in the nicho as you come in the front door, standing on a string of rose-shaped plastic lights. She's on my dashboard, or she dangles from a chain around my neck. Sometimes I see a quick flash of light in my mind's eye, and there she is like a logo. Even when my skies grow dark, and even when I am blind with fear, I can see her. Sometimes only in shadow, sometimes only in the farthest corner of my eye, but even when she is invisible, I know she's there.

Ana Consuelo Matiella was born in Nogales, Sonora, Mexico and raised in Ambos Nogales by a clan of Spaniards and Mexicans. Her fondest memories are of spending late Sonoran afternoons with her mothers, tías and madrinas, drinking café con leche, listening to their stories and trying to make sense of the world. Ana Consuelo is a fotonovela producer and health communications consultant. Her first book was *The Truth About Alicia and Other Stories*, a part of the Camino del Sol series published by the University of Arizona Press. This is her second book. Ana Consuelo divides her time between Santa Fe, New Mexico and Portland, Oregon.

Kali is an aspect of the great goddess Devi, the most complex and powerful of the goddesses. Kali is one of the fiercer aspects of Devi, but nonetheless as Shiva's consort, she represents female energy. Kali's aspect is destructive and all-pervading, as she represents the power or energy of time. Her four arms represent the four directions of space identified with the complete cycle of time. Kali is beyond time, beyond fear — her giving hand shows she is the giver of bliss. Because she represents a stage beyond all attachment, she appears fearful to us. So, she has a dual aspect— both destroyer of all that exists and the giver of eternal peace.

THIS IMAGE IS FROM DRAWINGS BY WOMEN OF MITHILA, INDIA.